CW01022349

THE LAST POTTER
OF BLACK BURTON

THE LAST POTTER OF BLACK BURTON

Richard Bateson and the potteries of Burton-in-Lonsdale

LEE CARTLEDGE

THE CHOIR PRESS

Copyright © 2021 Lee Cartledge

All rights reserved. No part of this publication may be reproduced or
transmitted in any form or by any means, electronic or mechanical
including photocopying, recording or any information storage or retrieval
system, without prior permission in writing from the publishers.

The right of Lee Cartledge to be identified as the author of this work has
been asserted by him in accordance with the Copyright,
Designs and Patents Act 1988

First published in the United Kingdom in 2021 by
The Choir Press

ISBN 978-1-78963-183-8

Map of Burton potteries c. 1850 design and production by Andrew Lathwell
www.lathwellcreative.com

Dedication

This book is dedicated to the memories of Richard Bateson and James "Jimmy" Skeates, two old potters who always had a lot to say.

Contents

Foreword

by Mark McKergow

As the grandson of Richard Bateson, I am delighted to see the publication of *The Last Potter of Black Burton*. Lee Cartledge, himself a highly skilled potter, has made a tremendous job of collecting information and materials not only about my grandfather but also covering the whole history of the pottery industry along the River Greta in Burton-in-Lonsdale.

Richard Bateson was indeed the last potter in Burton, and those who remember him personally are now fewer and fewer. Lee's work has therefore come at a crucial moment, when first-hand accounts can still just be connected with historical documentation. The pottery industry was key for this small community on the borders of Yorkshire, Lancashire and Cumbria for nearly three centuries until its demise in 1944. As this book shows, this was not quite the end of the story. Richard Bateson continued his career as a respected teacher of throwing in London and in Suffolk. He inspired a generation of potters and is fondly remembered by former students.

I don't really remember Grandpa as an active potter. By the time I was five years old he had retired and moved back north to Masongill, where there was an occasionally used electric wheel in the garage. There was no space for it in the little terraced house on Chapel Lane in Burton where he lived for the last 20 years of his life. He was active well into his 80's; always keen on a game of snooker or bowls. We walked down the hill and over the bridge to the bowling green and he would often point to the site of one former pottery or another. As a young teenager with a head full of rock music, I am sorry to say that I was less than curious. There was nothing left to see, and it all seemed to me like an imagined neverland.

Lee Cartledge has done us all proud by bringing this neverland back to life. Not only does he continue the pottery tradition of the area, he has assembled the most comprehensive collection of history, stories, first-hand accounts and photographs we are ever likely to see. This is social history of a high order: rooted in its context, explored by those who really understand how it was, and combining facts and figures with delightful vignettes of everyday life, the humour alongside the hard work.

In the pre-war years of the 20th century the Burton potteries were essentially continuing as they had for 200 years and more, with little recourse to modern technology – coal fired kilns, hand-mined clay, boys turning throwing wheels, to make pots for everyday storage and domestic use. Lee offers us a window onto this forgotten scene, bringing it to life with his personal experience, gift for a good story and no small amount of humour. This is a grand contribution to the history of Burton, the history of pottery and the story of rural arts in transformation from an industrial to a more artistic endeavour.

Mark McKergow
Edinburgh, Scotland
August 2020

Prologue

My family moved from Thornton Cleveleys to Oysterber Farm, on the outskirts of Low Bentham, North Yorkshire in 1976. My mother Kathy had previously run a small pottery in Thornton from a garage at the back of her house. But now, along with my father Barrie, they were energetically converting the farm buildings into a small pottery studio with a gallery open to the public. Thus, Bentham Pottery was born. Kathy worked full time in the pottery (and looked after my brother Paul and myself), producing a range of hand-thrown domestic wares whilst Barrie would produce more abstract hand-built pots when he could spare the time from his job.

Sometime in 1977, an old man in his eighties came into the pottery accompanied by his daughter and grandchildren. He shuffled in and introduced himself as Richard Timperley Bateson, the Last Potter of Black Burton, and asked my mother if he would be able to throw some pots on her pottery wheel in order to show his grandchildren what he had previously done when he had been working in the pottery industry. My mother obliged him, not sure what to expect, and let him have some clay. Within a few minutes it became apparent to my mother that Richard was an astoundingly good thrower. He could create forms and shapes on the wheel with a dexterity and fluidity that she had never seen before and she had attended quite a few pottery events where prestigious studio potters of the day had been demonstrating. Richard could handle both small and large weights of clay with equal skill and she was impressed with the rapidity with which he achieved his forms.

I can remember as a nine year old being dragged into the pottery to witness the Richard Bateson phenomenon and can remember even then being impressed with the skill on display. To my eternal regret, however, at that age he only held my attention for so long before I got distracted and was off out playing with my mates again. After this visit, Richard Bateson became a regular visitor to the pottery and he taught my mother a whole range of new techniques that improved the way she made her pots. In turn my mother has passed on these techniques to me and I am passing them on to my son.

Very regrettably we took no photos or videos of Richard throwing at Bentham Pottery. This was after all in the days before smart phones! However, we have a number of pots that Richard made at Bentham Pottery during this period and we treasure them.

At the time we really didn't appreciate the significance of Richard's visits. Obviously, Bentham Pottery benefited from his tuition, but I feel Richard handed the baton of the Burton pottery techniques to the next generation of local potters. Okay, he passed the skills on to the wrong village, (Low Bentham rather than Burton in Lonsdale), but you can't blame him for wanting to hand on these skills to a new generation.

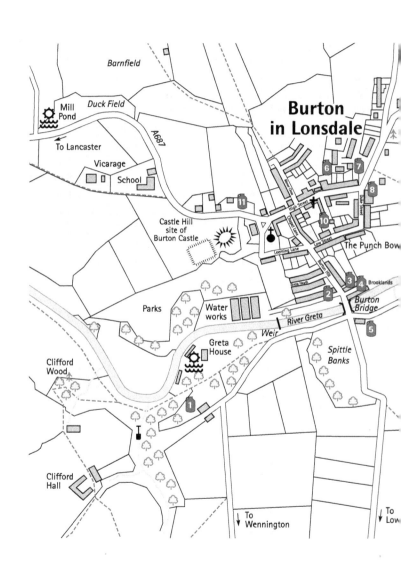

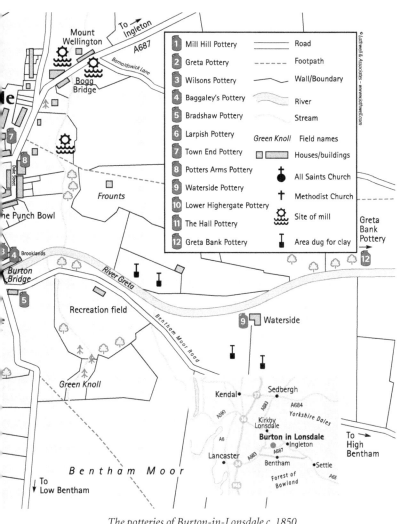

Key

1. Mill Hill Pottery
2. Greta Pottery
3. Wilsons Pottery
4. Baggaley's Pottery
5. Bradshaw Pottery
6. Larpish Pottery
7. Town End Pottery
8. Potters Arms Pottery
9. Waterside Pottery
10. Lower Highergate Pottery
11. The Hall Pottery
12. Greta Bank Pottery

Road
Footpath
Wall/Boundary
River
Stream
Green Knoll Field names
Houses/buildings
All Saints Church
Methodist Church
Site of mill
Area dug for clay

The potteries of Burton-in-Lonsdale c. 1850
(map by Andrew Lathwell Design)

CHAPTER ONE

Pottery in Black Burton

Burton-in-Lonsdale around 1870. The Bradshaw Pottery is clearly visible in the foreground, with Greta Pottery and Bridge End Pottery (Baggaley/Coates Pottery) behind.

Burton-in-Lonsdale, or Black Burton as it used to be called, has a long history of pottery making. Burton was ideally suited to pottery manufacture, as all the raw ingredients (clay, coal and water) were available in the locality. Pottery making in Burton can be traced back to the 1700s.

The Bateson family are deep rooted in the history of potteries in Burton. Certainly Richard's father, grandfather and great-grandfather were all involved in making pottery, not to mention numerous cousins and uncles.

Around 1900 there were five working potteries in Burton, namely: Waterside Pottery, Greta Pottery, Bridge End Pottery (Baggaley/Coates Pottery), Greta Bank Pottery and Town End Pottery. The early potteries at Burton produced hand thrown terracotta country pottery for the local farming community. These would have been household pots such as cooking pots, tableware and milk pans.

Around the 1840s stoneware pots began to be produced and the potteries experienced a large demand for stoneware bottles and jars for holding liquids from alcohol and fizzy pop to chemicals, pickles, jam and inks. This was helped by the railway coming to nearby High Bentham in 1840, which enabled a distribution of pots further afield. The stoneware bottle thus became one of the main products of the Burton potteries from this time, although more traditional earthenware pots were still produced.

Richard was born in 1894. I have little knowledge of what his early years were like, but can guess that they involved playing around Greta Woods and the River Greta, swimming at Topping Hole and at the Black Hole as well as playing in the clay pits and sliding down the Mill Hill clay bank (well that's what some of my childhood involved anyway!). Here are a couple of early memories in Richard's own words from a memoir he wrote in the 1970s;

> *"My first memory is of seeing workmen who were building two more kilns, making three in all. … My next recollection is of Father after tea making birds from the clay which had stuck to his shirt after he had been making big six-gallon bottles."*

Richard Bateson began work at Waterside Pottery at the age of 13 in 1907.

CHAPTER TWO

Waterside Pottery

The workers of Waterside Pottery in 1906.
Back row: (left to right) Harry Bateson (thrower and owner), Charlie Armer (general worker, night fireman), Jack Fisher (bench hand, day fireman), Bill Fletcher (carter), Jack Lee (wand weaver), Isaac Briscoe (general worker), Arthur Baines (packer), Ted Jones (miner), Sep Lee (thrower), John B Brayshaw (namer and kiln loader), Jack Fletcher (carter).
Middle row: (left to right) Bill Standing (fettler and kiln loader), Sam Skeats (engine driver), Jim Brayshaw (jnr) (turner, day fireman), Squire Taylor (wand weaver mainly, but could do any job in the pottery), Jim Brayshaw (snr) (wand weaver), Teddy Tomlinson (miner), Christopher Isaac Briscoe (naming, kiln loader, night fireman), Dixon Bateson (general worker).
Front row: (left to right) Charlie Brayshaw (bench hand, taker off), Richard T Bateson (this was the year before Richard began work), Gordon Taylor (general worker), Harold Bateson (jam jar maker).
Richard Bateson is in the front row with his hand covering his neck. Apparently he'd broken his top button and didn't want his Mum to see it in this Lancaster Guardian photograph. Where was Frank Bateson on this day?

Waterside Pottery was located diagonally opposite the football field in Burton, alongside the River Greta. Its main product prior to the First World War was stoneware bottles. The pottery had three kilns incorporated into a two-storey building. It employed 30 or so men. They worked an eleven hour day, starting at 6.00 am and finishing at 5.00pm. Breakfast was between 8.00am until 8.30am and they had a one hour lunch break from 12.30 until 1.30. Saturday was a half-day so work ceased at noon.

Waterside Pottery traded under the name of William Bateson & Sons. William died in 1892, leaving the pottery to his three sons, Henry (Richard's father – who was also known as Harry), Robert and Frank.

Robert fell out with his two brothers over the running of the pottery as he felt that it wasn't modern enough and needed to update its equipment, techniques and processes. History would prove his thinking correct on these points. Henry and Frank bought out Robert's share of William Bateson & Sons and, with this money, Robert bought Greta Pottery from Thomas Coates in 1902 and set up on his own.

The Two Bosses

Harry (Henry) Bateson

Harry Bateson was Richard Bateson's father. Harry, as well as being the joint boss with Frank, was the main thrower. He was a respected and liked man; he was very hard working and led by example. Harry's philosophy to work at the pottery was "If tha' makes pots, workers will look after 'em". I'm guessing the worker had no option but to look after them, because you had to keep up with the boss and there was no getting away from the fact that Harry was in the thick of it in the heart of the pottery workshop, sat at his wheel and effectively creating the tempo of the work with his own hands. There was no way anyone could shirk work in that situation. Harry was a phenomenal thrower. He could throw 120 six-gallon bottles in a day. The clay required to make a six-gallon bottle was 66lbs, which from a thrower's perspective is

Photo taken around 1890. (left to right) James Brayshaw, Frank Bateson, Jack Lee, William Taylor (Squire's father), Harry Bateson (Richard's father) and Squire Taylor.

an excessively large amount of clay. When Harry was throwing the six-gallon bottle, his whole arm would disappear into the pot, with the rim nestled in his armpit.

Harry was a man of few words. Richard can only remember him raising his voice to him once and that incident happened after Richard got into a fight with another pottery worker called Kenneth Firth. I don't know how the fight started, but the end result is that Kenneth was lifted up by Richard with his arm between his legs and thrown head first into one of the large brewing vats that they used for glazing (thankfully only partly filled). Kenneth managed to extract himself from the vat, and, covered from head to toe in white liquid glaze, ran into the throwing workshop to complain to Harry about Richard. Kenneth elaborated the story to Harry somewhat, by saying that he had been knocked out in the vat for 3 minutes, although how an unconscious man can time three minutes is anybody's guess. Harry left his wheel and went to confront Richard in a terrible rage and came out with the classic line "What tha' hell hast tha' thrown what's-his-name in the what's-it-called-for?", to which Richard replied "He was looking in the vat leaning over and just fell in" and that, as they say, was the end of it and the extent of

Harry's wrath. I can only guess Kenneth must have been sent home to get changed as it would be extremely uncomfortable walking around wearing a layer of glaze, not to mention the health and safety implications!

Such was Harry's dedication to pottery that, on his regular Sunday walk with his family, he would always carry a trowel with him, in case their walk took them past any likely source of clay that may prove to be of use at some future date. He would gather a small piece of clay with the trowel and fire it in one of the kilns to check its properties.

FRANK BATESON

Frank was joint owner of Waterside Pottery with his brother Harry. Frank originally trained as a chemist and worked in the chemist's shop in Kirkby Lonsdale. He was drawn into the pottery when his father died in 1892 and he inherited his share of the company. Frank was more of a conventional boss, in the sense that he was a white collar worker, unlike Harry, who was immersed in the pottery workshop. Frank dealt with customers and orders and did the necessary paper work for the business. He travelled around the north of England to find new customers and renew long-standing orders. He also went to Ireland four times a year for the same purpose.

To the young Richard Bateson, Frank never seemed to do any work, other than count bottles. Frank seemed to have an uncanny ability to appear out of nowhere usually just as Richard was about to enact some prank, which made him feel Frank was a 'peeping Tom'. Richard always had the uneasy feeling that Frank thought he had no right to be at the pottery. Richard explains this as the reason he used to play tricks on Frank, a favourite being filling his pipe with clay when he wasn't looking. Frank, like Harry, was a man of few words. According to Richard he would only ever say "Yes", "No", or turn his back on you. Richard could not imagine him as being much good in any negotiations as he could barely string a sentence together. If it came to any competition from any other pottery Richard felt that, rather than negotiate, Frank would just drop the price and, as such, Richard felt that Waterside Pottery was working harder than it really had to, to make ends meet. That said, Frank did manage to keep the pottery going from 1892 (when his father died) until 1933.

I think part of the success of Harry and Frank as the bosses was down to the "good cop/bad cop" routine they had going on. Harry would keep the men working hard and efficiently whilst at the same time Frank would keep them slightly on their toes.

Richard begins work at Waterside Pottery

Waterside Pottery was booming in 1907. The pottery was struggling to keep up with all the orders they were getting. Two older workers left the pottery at this time, which caused a series of promotions within the workforce. This resulted in vacancies in some of the lesser skilled jobs, noticeably there was no longer anybody operating one of the jam jar making machines. Harry, for whatever reason, decided to pull Richard out of Bentham Grammar School at the age of 13 to work at the pottery as a jam jar maker. I'm not sure whether the decision was based upon how well Richard was doing at the grammar school or whether they couldn't find anybody else to do the job for the measly three shillings a week they were offering or even if Harry recognised Richard's hand/eye coordination skills were perfect for pottery work. Richard's other siblings carried on at school, which must have been hard for him at times. Here are some of Richard's thoughts about this taken from his memoir:

"*I was not a brilliant scholar by any means – I enjoyed games too much! At the end of the last term, Father said, "I want you in the pottery". Although I was only thirteen years old in March, and rather small – yet fairly strong.*"...

"*My first year at the Waterside Pottery was not a great success. In the holidays, I could see my brothers going up the river fishing and having a jolly good time, and I, the poor relation, was making jam-jars in the muck and sludge and smoke. I think on the whole I must have taken advantage of my position of the son of the boss. Although I worked fairly hard, I gave the workmen a rather weary time. Often my father, who was throwing downstairs, would shout about the scuffling that was going on up there."*

The jam jars were made on a steam-powered machine called a 'jigger and jolly'. This would have been a modern piece of equipment at the time and it enabled a relatively unskilled person to repeatedly make the same pot. A plaster mould with the external shape of the pot would be inserted into a metal cup. A pre-weighed piece of clay would then be thrown into the plaster mould and the cup and mould would spin. A template of the internal shape would then be lowered into the mould, forming the pot, or jam jar in this case. The pot would dry a bit in the mould before being emptied out.

There were three jigger and jolly machines at Waterside Pottery exclusively used for making 2lb, 3lb, and 4lb jam jars. Richard worked on these machines alongside James Skeates and Harold Bateson (Frank's son), all lads of similar age. Between the three of them they would produce several thousand jam jars per week. The main customer for the jars was a jam factory at Wigton run by the Cartwright family. It would have been very repetitive work. According to James Skeates it was one of the worst jobs in the pottery. "It was hard work and would scour the skin off your hands." The jam jars were very handy for filling the kilns with, as they fitted in the gaps between the bottles, so this meant that no kiln space was wasted.

Richard was very glad when after a year of making jam jars he was promoted to another job.

CHAPTER THREE

Winning the clay and making the pots

Undoubtedly the reason for the location of Waterside Pottery was that it had opencast coal and opencast stoneware clay in the field adjacent to the pottery. I'm not sure when the coal ran out, but the clay ran out in 1905. This forced the potters to open a drift mine to access a 4 foot 6 inch seam of stoneware clay that ran into the hillside. Ted Tomlinson was employed as the clay miner. Ted had worked at Ingleton Colliery. He dug the clay in the mine whilst another Ted, Ted "Gunner" Jones, carted the clay from the mine to the pottery. A railway line was eventually built from the pottery into the mine to make this task easier. Above the clay seam, there was a 6 inch seam of coal. This coal was used to fuel the steam engine that powered all the pottery machinery. As a special privilege, the miner was allowed to take some of this coal back home with him. Richard recalled how, "The clay in its natural state was as hard as rock. The miner's picks had to be sharpened every day".

Terracotta clay was, and still is, available opencast at Mill Hill near to Greeta House. Terracotta clay is normally red in colour; the Burton terracotta is unique in being black in colour. I am reliably informed that it is black due to having oil trapped in it. The clay, though, does fire to red like ordinary terracotta. The Burton potters referred to this clay as 'blackware' because of its appearance. I have always wondered if the origin of the name Black Burton is due to the colour of the terracotta found there.

Waterside Pottery predominantly used the stoneware clay, but they would at times use some of the 'blackware'. All the Burton potteries had free access to the 'blackware' and I think even now anybody living in Burton has the rights to dig it.

Above: *James Singleton in the clay mine in 1940.*

Left: *Clay mine at Waterside Pottery around 1940. Jack Wilson pushing the barrow.*

Processing the Clay

The Burton clay is compacted shale, which takes a lot of breaking down. Once dug, the clay was left in piles for at least one year, although preferably for two years. This allowed the winter frosts to 'weather' the clay and break it down somewhat. The clay was then totally broken down in a blunger. A blunger is like a large-scale steam powered Kenwood Chef mixer that mixed the clay with a paddle. Water was added with the clay shale and, over a few hours, it would turn the shale and water into a thick liquid slip. It would then be sieved into a clay settling pan. Sieving would get rid of any undesirable foreign bodies such as iron from the clay. A clay pan is like a shallow swimming pool where the clay would be left to dry. Once the clay was considered dry enough, it would then be dug out of the clay pan and left to dry on the walls of the pan, before being stored in the pottery. Wet cloths would have been placed over the stored clay to prevent it from drying further.

Jack Telford operating the blunger in 1940.

Jack Telford filling a clay settling pan with Burton 'blackware' in 1940.

Clay drying on the walls of a clay pan at Waterside pottery around 1912. (Left to right) Harry Bateson, Dixon Bateson, unknown.

One of Richard's nephews, Jeff Bateson, called in at Bentham Pottery and regaled us with the tale of when he went to visit Waterside Pottery as a young lad. Whilst wandering around the pottery, one of the workers challenged him to a race across one of the clay pans. Now young Jeff had no notion of what a clay pan was. To him it just looked like a walled area with a solid earth floor. Clay in a clay pan dries from the outside to the centre, so whilst it may be possible to stand on the clay close to the outside wall, the clay in the middle can be rather on the soft side. I guess you can tell where this tale is going? The pottery worker just stood still and poor Jeff ran at breakneck speed into a gooey mess in the middle and got a right telling off from his mother when he got home!

The process of blunging and drying the clay was mainly done in the spring, so the clay could dry out during the summer. They would endeavour to prepare enough clay to last a whole year. Prior to being thrown, the clay would be mixed up again in another machine called a pug mill to ensure an even consistency and make it perfect for throwing.

Charlie Armer operating the pug mill in 1940.

Pottery Production

"When I first began work, we had two regular throwers, and it is difficult to believe the speed at which these two men worked. It was always fascinating to watch a five- or six-gallon bottle being made in the time of four or five minutes. One lift or course to the cylinder, and one knuckling course to the full lift and width to the gauge; leaving a sufficient roll of clay to run in the top and make the neck. The width of the corkhole was gauged by the fingers: two fingers' width for the ordinary bottle, and three fingers' width for a treacle-jar. The amount of clay required was approximately five pounds for a half-gallon, eleven pounds or a Hyndburn brick for one gallon, and an extra brick for each of the succeeding gallons up to the six-gallon bottles. I have managed to make up to ten gallons, just once for a special order." (From Richard's memoir)

When Richard began work in 1907, Waterside Pottery had two throwers; Harry Bateson (Richard's father) and Sep Lee. One kiln required 1200 one-gallon bottles or their equivalent to fill it. Prior to the First World War, two and occasionally three kilns were fired per week. This meant that these two throwers had to make 2,400-3,600 one-gallon bottles or their equivalent between them per week. Given that the clay required to throw a one-gallon bottle is 11lb, this means they were throwing between 12 tons and 18 tons of clay per week! At Bentham Pottery we tend to get through 4 tons per year (Our main pot though is the 12oz mug, not the 11lb gallon bottle). During one particularly busy period in 1907, three kilns were fired each week for thirteen weeks. The main customer during this period was apparently Guinness in Ireland, where the bottles were required for stout.

The throwers were helped in their task by the other workmen. A 'bench hand or 'wedger' would weigh out the ball of clay and 'wedge' and hand knead it to take out any air bubbles before presenting the ball to the thrower. Once the pot was thrown, another man known as a 'taker off' would wire the pot and lift it off the wheel onto a ware board. Once the ware boards were full, the 'taker off' would transport the whole board to a gantry in the kiln room where the pots would begin to dry.

The lads operating the jigger and jolly machines for making the jam jars would take the clay straight from the pug mill and wire it into segments for placing into the machine.

The largest bottle made at Waterside Pottery was the six-gallon bottle. This 'beast' of a pot required two men to lift it off the wheel. The six-gallon bottles were moved about by picking them up by the neck; this method worked fine provided there was no moisture in the clay. If the clay was still even slightly wet the unfortunate carrier would be left holding a bottle neck minus the bottle and be in very grave danger from an irate thrower. Apparently it wasn't uncommon for workers having done this and, providing nobody had seen them, to quickly wet the neck and do a fast bodge repair job so the next person to lift the bottle would get the blame. All the workers in turn probably did this bodging until someone was caught red handed!

Richard Bateson throwing in 1940.

Jack Coates throwing at the Coates Pottery (Bridge End) in 1920.

Once the pots had dried sufficiently, they were put back on the wheel and turned. Turning involves shaving off the wall thickness using sharp edged tools. Pots, especially bottle shapes, tend to be a bit thick around the base when thrown, so turning would remove this weight. Also, the thrower's knuckle tends to leave a spiral groove up the pot. It was felt that this spiral groove needed to be removed with turning tools to make the pot look 'industrially' made. Ironically the explosion in craft pottery after the war encouraged leaving the spiral grooves on pots, so that they *looked* hand made.

Handles could then be added if required. Some bottles required screw tops; these would be made at this point using special moulds and dies. The company purchasing the bottles usually insisted that the bottle had the name of the company and contents clearly visible on the surface of the pot. These details would be stamped into the bottle after turning.

The pots, when totally dry, were ready for glazing. Jim Brayshaw mixed up the glaze in the large brewing vats, one of the ones into which Richard had thrown Kenneth. The glaze consisted of the stoneware clay, flint, whiting and Cornish stone, similar to what we use at Bentham pottery today. Jim would mix the glaze in eight-gallon batches. It must have been quite a responsible job because if you got it wrong it would affect all the pots in the kilns. I would guess that they would have two batches mixed at any one time, so a batch could be tested prior to using it on a lot of pots. Manganese or iron was added to some of this glaze and the tops of the bottles would be dipped into this mixture to give the bottles their 'copper' tops. Once glazed the pots would have to dry out again before loading into the kiln.

Glazing, or applying white slip, to milk pans at Coates Pottery around 1910. Thomas Coates (left) and Jack Coates.

The pots were stacked on shelves with props separating the shelves. The top of the kiln was reserved for the large five- and six-gallon bottles. After the kiln was filled its mouth or opening was bricked up and the eight fire mouths were lit.

Firing the Kilns

Firing lasted between 50 and 60 hours depending upon how densely packed the kilns were. One kiln required twelve tons of coal to fire it. There was a weekly firing routine. The kilns were always emptied on the Monday then they were packed from late Monday afternoon until Wednesday morning. The fire mouths were then lit; firing had begun. Firing would be finished by Friday night and over the weekend the kilns would cool.

Twenty-four-hour attention was necessary whilst firing. There was a day fireman and a night fireman. It was their job to continually stoke the fire mouths of the kiln, watch out for any outbreaks of fire and to monitor the temperature.

The kilns at Waterside were not kept in very good condition:

"Frequently the kiln was in such a condition that the red heat from the inside of the kiln used to come through and you could see it. Workmen used to light their pipes with it!"

Not surprisingly fires broke out. The two-inch-thick floorboards on the top floor of the pottery often sprung up in flame near to the kiln. The fireman would put the fire out with a bucket of water. There is no record of a Burton pottery burning down.

The kilns had to reach 1280 degrees centigrade for the glaze ingredients to melt and form the glaze. The kilns had small test pots at the bottom and top. These diminutive pots could be taken out of small openings, using metal rods to ascertain sufficient firing.

During the winter months the kilns attracted tramps from around the area like moths to a flame to take advantage of this 'free' heat. Richard can remember having to step over these sleeping tramps when his dad had asked him to go down to the pottery late at night to check on the firing progress and reassure him that the pottery wasn't ablaze.

When firing, the kilns made the whole pottery uncomfortably hot, and they leaked smoke and sulphur into the work rooms. It got so bad that "You couldn't see your hand in front of you". The top floor got the worst of it. "Anyone working upstairs was coughing and spluttering all day. All the windows in the pottery had to be left open to make it tolerable."

The kilns were unpacked on a Monday. The pots, even after a weekend cooling, were still hot. However, they had to be unpacked to keep to the weekly schedule. The absolute worst job in the pottery was taking the top row of pots out of the kiln. One man would do this each week and they would take it in turn every week. After about two minutes of working at the top of the kiln passing bottles down in intense heat they had to emerge from the kiln covered in sweat and have a rest. All the other men would sit down and wait for this man to recover before he went in again to get some more pots out.

Richard Bateson and James Skeates discussing this years later couldn't really work out why another man couldn't have gone into the kiln whilst the first man was resting, as it would have been far more productive than the whole team sitting down whilst the one man recovered. The kiln got easier to unload and less hot the more pots and shelves were taken out. Larger pots had to be wrapped in sacks when they were taken out of the kiln, as the sudden cooling would crack them.

When the pots had cooled down to room temperature, they were tested. They were dipped in a bucket of water and blown into. If any air bubbles rose and floated to the surface, the pot had 'dunted' and would not hold fluid. The Burton potters had a great way of disposing of these pots. They simply threw them *en masse* into the River Greta, which is why you can still find broken sections of stoneware bottles in the river, although there aren't as many now as in the 1970s when we first moved to the area, as a lot of them have been washed downstream.

Harry Capstick firing the kiln in 1940.

Charlie Armer inside one of the kilns, 1940.

The Wand Weavers

The large pots were encased in cane baskets. This was the bubble wrap of the day and would protect the bottles from breakage. Squire Taylor and Jack Lee were the main basket makers or 'wand weavers' as they were called. Squire and Jack worked in a small building outside the main pottery. Some of the cane was actually grown at Waterside, though most was imported. The basket casings on bottles would eventually wear out, so old bottles were sometimes returned for re-casing. It was always a popular job taking the old casings off bottles that had been used in public houses for holding alcohol, because if they were stored under the bar, it was quite common for any falling coins to get lodged and stuck into the weave of the basket. These coins would reveal themselves when the old baskets were taken off.

Jack Lee weaving around 1930.

Distributing the pots

Peter Bateson (Richard's brother) around 1920.

Waterside Pottery had four horses and carts. Jack and Bill Fletcher, a father and son team, were employed as carters by Waterside Pottery. They would help load the four carts up with pots and take them to the railway station at High Bentham. Each man controlled two carts in a line. At the station they would unload the pots onto the goods wagon and then fill the cart with coal for firing the kilns before doing the return trip. Two trips were done a day, bringing back 6 tons of coal. A lot of pots were lost due to the train shunting into the goods wagon and jolting the pots (despite the fact that the pots were well packed). There were a lot less breakages when pots were taken by road rather than train after the First World War.

I'm not sure where the four horses were stabled, but the pottery had a piece of land on the opposite side of the river at Barnoldswick that yielded hay for the horses. Every year the pottery workers would abandon pots and kilns for a day and would descend upon the field fuelled with kegs of beer provided by Frank and Harry and gather the hay in; it must have been a refreshing change of scene for them.

"The first hill on the way to Bentham was Skipton Gate. In places this is about 1-in-4, or 1-in-5. The horses, loaded as they always were, took a zigzag course up the hill in slants of about forty-five degrees, three or four times before reaching the top. Thus, there was a zigzag horse track, on which the surface was broken, so that the animals had a firm grip for their shoes. They came back to the same course when empty, but of course if they were loaded, the carter would put on the handbrake. We could hear the screech of the brakes as they came down the hill. Father, who was nearly always at the potter's wheel, would send one of us to open the wide doors, so that no time would be lost, and the carts could be backed direct to the appropriate places for firing the kilns. The horses would back, and would stand almost in front of a fire-mouth, and out slid nearly a ton of coal. I cannot remember that there was ever a mishap with any of the horses, even when we had to get fresh horsemen." (From Richard's memoir)

Potters hay timing around 1910. (Left to right) Back row; Gordon Taylor, Charlie Brayshaw, Squire Taylor. Middle row; Unknown, unknown, Charlie Armer, unknown, Ted Tomlinson, Dickson Bateson, unknown. Front row; Unknown, Eric Bateson, Molly Bateson.

CHAPTER FOUR

Richard's progression through the pottery

"I was always fascinated watching the thrower making pots, and during their break times I would ask if it was possible to have a go. I seemed to pick up the rhythm and control fairly quickly, and by the end of the year I was myself throwing four-pound jars, wages four shillings per week. For the first three years I never received a penny wage for myself – I was forced to make a few things for myself and sell them without my Uncle Frank's knowledge." (From Richard's memoir)

After 12 months of making jam jars, Richard was promoted to a turner, which was a far better job. He enjoyed sitting at the wheel turning bottles and this motivated him to want to learn how to throw pots on the wheel. Harry was keen to encourage Richard to start throwing, so on occasions, he would get Richard to 'take off' for him, enabling Richard to see how Harry was forming the clay on the wheel and the necessary differing speeds of the wheel. Richard started practising throwing at every opportunity he had, either during the working day, or after work hours, providing a wheel was free and the steam engine was still running. Harry and Sep (the other thrower) would occasionally help him with this, offering advice and direction. It quickly became apparent that Richard had a natural ability for throwing and within a few months he was making small bottles that were good enough for selling. Richard then started attempting to make the larger bottle sizes, from a quarter gallon to half gallons up to one-gallon bottles. Some throwers never actually progressed beyond the 11lb of clay required to make a one-gallon bottle. I'm sure I would have stopped there, as 11lbs of clay is really close to

my limit. By the end of his second year at Waterside Pottery
Richard was practically throwing full time and his skills rapidly
improved. He quickly continued working up the bottle sizes and
by the age of 17 he could throw any pot that Waterside Pottery
produced, even the dreaded six-gallon bottle.

> *"A boy was not chosen and then trained as a thrower. Boys
> had endless opportunities for watching the potters at work and
> if one had the interest in his blood he would jump to the wheel
> while it was idle during a break and try his hand. If he showed
> promise he would get practice and advice. Richard Bateson
> was just such a boy in the early years of the century. His
> promise brought him the offer of a scholarship to Wedgewood's
> where he would have learned more sophisticated potting than
> Burton could have taught him. And his promise too made his
> Father reject the offer. Good throwers were not easily come by
> and were worth more than their salt. So at Burton he stayed-
> first at Waterside and then Bridge End – throwing pots from 6
> in the morning until 5.00 in the evening. Even though the
> thrower worked sitting down at the wheel it was repetitive and
> tiring work. In the drowsiness of the early afternoon he would
> sometimes "fall – asleep" while throwing a pot to wake up and
> find himself at the gauge of the shoulder." (This quote is taken
> from a Lancaster university paper, Prospects, 'Lonsdale Potters
> Then and Now', November 1965. The author is unknown. The
> extract is from an interview with Richard Bateson in 1965.)*

Prior to the First World War, the highest paid worker at Waterside
Pottery was the thrower Sep Lee. Sep took home 28 shillings per
week. Other semi-skilled workers were paid no more than 22
shillings. Richard's wage, by contrast, was a mere three shillings;
this went up to four shillings in his second year. However, this
really meant nothing to Richard as he didn't get to see any of the
money as it all went back home, so he started making hot water
bottles after work hours and selling them. On a good week
Richard could make 10 shillings from selling these hot water

bottles. This was the only money that Richard got from the pottery prior to the First World War. Frank apparently disapproved of this, but it was in Frank's nature to disapprove of things.

Larking about

The morale amongst the workers at Waterside Pottery was good. They would always have time for a bit of fun, although not everybody always saw the funny side of some of the antics that went on.

Throwing clay around was a common activity among the younger workers and sometimes the older workers, who perhaps should have known better, joined in. Anybody holding a lamp (some of the workshop space would have been dark), was at risk of the lamp suddenly flying from their hands, due to a well-aimed ball of clay hitting it. This could then fuel a revenge attack. I think having Harry in the main workshop probably prevented any escalations of this activity.

> "There was no such thing as electric power – we made our own lamps. Only the throwers had the paraffin lamps with a lamp-glass. The rest of the workers had either candles or the old-fashioned type of container with a cotton wick. I had always been good at ball games and I used to be able to hit with a piece of leather-hard clay anything I thought fit to aim at. The men's lamps would suddenly fly through the air just like a comet, oil and flame following the container. I was often caught – and then I had a rough time." (From Richard's memoir)

Villagers would sometimes bring pieces of limestone to the pottery to be fired in a pot. This would create quick lime, which was commonly used as whitewash for painting buildings. Once fired, the villager would return with a bucket and collect the quick lime powder. On occasions, water was added to the quick lime without the villager knowing. This water created a chemical reaction which gradually heated the quick lime and caused it to expand and boil. This reaction tended to become visible just as the unfortunate villager was about to leave the driveway of Waterside Pottery, with a vapour trail of steam following them from the bucket.

If there were any milking cows in the fields close to the road on the way to the pottery, Richard would, on occasion, climb over a fence and squeeze and aim one of the cow's teats over the hedge to spray unsuspecting pottery workers on the way into work.

If a worker came into work late (and I guess one of the advantages to coming in late was their clothes wouldn't be streaked with warm cow's milk) then they would be applauded as they entered the building. If the same person was late over consecutive days, then a 'jazz band' would come down the driveway to meet them, comprising men banging crow bars, pokers and tins together. Harry Bateson was known to occasionally join in with this (and enjoy it). It depended on what side of the bed the recipient got out of as to how well the 'jazz band' was received.

Samuel Skeates was the pottery engineer. He looked after all the machinery and the steam engine that powered everything. He started work half an hour before everybody else to ensure steam was up, so work could begin at 6.00am. There were a lot of bearings throughout the pottery that on occasion would start to squeak, so Sam would wander round with a little step ladder and apply oil on what he thought was the squeaky bearing. Richard, sat at the pottery wheel, discovered that he could make the exact sound of the bearing squeak by whistling and he often led poor Sam on a wild goose chase going up and down his ladder with a can of oil trying to locate where the squeak was coming from.

The top floor of the pottery was made of two-inch thick planks, with a slight gap between the planks. Richard discovered that if you filled an unfired bottle with water and left it directly above where somebody was working in the room below, then after 5 or 10 minutes, the bottle would soften and suddenly let out a flood of water. The beauty of this time lag is that you could be downstairs talking (from a distance) with the unfortunate victim when the dam burst. The water coming out of the bottle was never as clean as the water that went in.

Working Conditions

Workers at Waterside Pottery sometime around 1900. Notice the hand crank on the wheel, which allowed pots to be made when the steam engine wasn't running. Jack Lee's peg leg is visible on the far left. (Left to Right) Jack Lee, Squire Taylor, Unknown, Unknown, Unknown, Harry Bateson, Unknown, William Taylor, Unknown, Frank Bateson. Seated Unknown.

The working conditions at Waterside Pottery were, by modern standards, extremely poor and imposed a grave danger to health. The conditions would not be tolerated today thankfully due to trade unions and health and safety directives. Prior to the First World War, Waterside Pottery had neither.

The atmosphere in the pottery buildings, as mentioned, was particularly unpleasant whilst kilns were firing and being unloaded. Worst of all, the raw materials for the glazes were handled loose without using protective face masks. Flint dust, which is pure silica, escaped into the atmosphere, and was responsible for causing silicosis, a major killer in the pottery industry at the time. Kiln packers were particularly prone to silicosis, as they would dust the kiln shelves with flint to prevent pots from sticking to the shelves during firing. They would also sweep the flint dust off the shelves after firing. A lot of this flint would inevitably get into the kiln packers' lungs. Richard can remember his brother Peter, a kiln packer who died of silicosis, coming out of the kiln and "sitting in the wanding-house, and coughing his heart up, due to the silicosis dust". Richard could reel off lists of the men that had died of silicosis at Waterside Pottery.

Richard Bateson throwing at Waterside Pottery in the 1930s.

The problem was basically ignorance of the dangers of the chemicals. No one realised they were responsible for so many deaths. It wouldn't have been difficult to make the chemicals safe through proper handling and sadly many died through unsafe practice.

The pottery was also full of potentially lethal apparatus. Photographs show that engine workings were neither protected nor fenced off. Bert Williams, a deaf boy who worked at Waterside Pottery, got his chest trapped under a hoist. Fortunately, he was seen and the hoist was raised. However, he was off work for several weeks and never fully recovered.

In the winter months, particularly if a kiln wasn't firing, the clay could be very cold. Thomas Chapels, who worked as a bench hand, can remember "after wedging the clay you could clench your fists, and they would bleed due to chapped skin". The cold clay also affected the throwers. Richard describes it well; "It was like trying to throw a snowball. Your arms went numb."

Given all this is it any wonder that Richard ran away and joined the army at the start of the First World War?

CHAPTER FIVE

Richard goes to war

Richard dressed in uniform.

The First World War was declared on the 4th August 1914. Richard was very keen to join up and take part in this great adventure, which was in danger of all being over by Christmas. He saw it as the "only chance of getting out of a village and seeing the rest of the world". He was also aware that Harry probably would not be too happy about him leaving the business and going off to war.

Richard's brother Kenyon was going out with a nurse at the time who lived in Wigan and he was going to visit her for a long weekend. Richard asked Kenyon to let him know if he found out any way of joining up whilst he was there. Richard got a telegram from Kenyon at the pottery on the Friday, which he managed to intercept before anybody else could read it. The telegram said "Come at once, East Lancashire Division going to Egypt". Richard decided to keep this a secret and so on the Monday morning he got up, put on his work clothes, had a bite to eat with his dad and then hung fire until Harry walked off to work. Richard then ran back upstairs, got changed, walked to Bentham Station and caught the train to Wigan where he met up with Kenyon. By 12.30 they were both in uniform enlisted to the 5th Manchester Regiment, literally one month after war had been declared. I would be fascinated to know how Richards's parents reacted to this when they subsequently found out.

I'm sure another book could be written about Richard's war experiences, but this one is about his pottery career. Suffice to say he fought in Gallipoli where he took a bullet in his wrist, and he fought in France at Passchendaele where he got injured from a piece of shrapnel in the groin. This meant he was back at Burton recovering when peace was declared in 1918. It was around this time that Richard made one of the better decisions in his life, and he proposed to his childhood sweetheart Annie Elizabeth Pedder. They were married 12 months after peace had been declared on 10 November 1919. They were to have three children and live to celebrate a rare platinum wedding anniversary (70 years).

Waterside Pottery during and after the First World War

The pottery lost a lot of workers due to the war effort. Some of the older men who had retired came back to the pottery to help out. Richard's sister and sister in law, Mabel and Millie, came into the pottery to operate the jam jar machines. Richard can remember being "rather horrified to think of women in the pottery" when he found out whilst he was in the army. Richard was concerned not just about the dirty conditions in the pottery, but also the foul language used by the potters! Production though did continue throughout the whole war period, albeit on a reduced scale.

After the war not all the men that had worked at the pottery prior to 1914 came back to work. In fact the workforce never again exceeded the boom years of the pre-war period. This was probably just as well as demand had slowed down quite a bit; instead of firing two or three kilns per week prior to the war, they were now firing one and only occasionally two kilns.

Richard began throwing again as soon as he was demobbed. It must have been strange for him after five years of army life coming back to full time throwing. Richard was now paid 24 shillings a week. This must have upset Frank no end.

Business continued. A basket making company called Hunts started ordering all sizes of bottles from them. I suspect Hunts were buying the bottles from Waterside Pottery and casing them themselves before passing them on to their customers. Mabie Todd, a pen and ink manufacturer, gave them some large orders for ink bottles. The United Alkali Company started ordering bottles for storing chemicals. The British Navy ordered large amounts of 14lb pickle jars and 10lb jam jars. Drink manufacturers from Ireland continued ordering bottles.

At some point during the war Waterside Pottery took on a new thrower; one Frederick Slater.

Freddie Slater

Freddie was a good thrower. I mean he must have been really good, because Richard rated him highly. Freddie had learnt to throw at Town End Pottery in Burton under the guidance of the pottery owner, Jacky Parker. When Jacky died in 1908, Freddie borrowed money and bought Town End Pottery. However, despite Freddie being a brilliant thrower he wasn't great at business. According to Richard Bateson, he was "too busy advising other people how to run their businesses, instead of running his own". Freddie only lasted three or four years before going bankrupt just before the First World War. Freddie then moved out of Burton and got a job at Portobello Pottery in Edinburgh. His family stayed in Burton though, which probably explains why he moved back to Burton as soon as he could.

Freddie discovered lots of new pottery techniques in Edinburgh. He also discovered health and safety regulations and trade unions. Now, Freddie was a strong unwieldy character. In Richard's words, "He was lord of all he surveyed". He was particularly "Boss of all he surveyed in throwing". Freddie would always get the bench hands to weigh slightly less clay than the other throwers for making the same pots, just to prove he was the better potter and could make the same pot with less weight of clay and frustratingly he always could. He was fiercely competitive at 'chasing' the other throwers when they were making the same pots. Freddie always wanted to be in front of the other throwers in terms of throwing speed and volumes of pots made. Richard can remember Freddie once making a batch of thin based bottles, which meant that when they came to glaze the bottles, the bases absorbed too much water and collapsed. Richard turned to Freddie and said "Na then Freddie, tha's losing tha grip". Freddie didn't like that at all!

Freddie brought some of the new techniques that he'd learnt in Edinburgh back to Burton. He introduced a technique of using templates to finish off the shoulders and necks of bottles, so they didn't need turning. This would have saved a considerable amount of time. He also introduced trade unions to Waterside Pottery. He established himself as the union representative and talked as many workers into joining the union as he could. Richard didn't join. I guess he owed his loyalties to his Dad. Freddie then went on to organise a short strike to protest against the health and safety conditions at Waterside Pottery. This has to be seen as a brave move on Freddie's part. I'm sure it would have been easier to orchestrate were it not for the fact that Harry himself was sat in the middle of the pottery surrounded by the health and safety conditions Freddie was objecting to. Freddie was, in actual fact, quite right to object to the conditions. Certainly the conditions at Waterside Pottery would not be tolerated today and for good reason. It's just at the time the owners and workforce had little idea that there *was* a health and safety problem.

Richard can remember Freddie paying off the union members during this short strike. The whole thing culminated in a meeting on neutral ground in the Sunday School in Burton, where Freddie, Harry, Frank, representatives of the union and a man from the ministry were present. Freddie began the meeting by telling everyone how much better things were at Portobello Pottery, and then went on at length continuing along the same theme. Eventually an exasperated Harry stood up and said "I'm surprised if it's such a wonderful place that Mr Slater didn't stay there". At that point the man from the ministry squashed the comment and deleted it from the records and advised them to continue in a civil manner. I'm not sure what health and safety improvements Freddie managed to establish, but they must have come to some agreement, because the strike was called off and Freddie continued to work at the pottery. In truth they would have been very reluctant to lose a thrower of Freddie's calibre, and on balance Freddie's good points just about outweighed his bad points.

During the 1920s Freddie managed to convince Frank into using the 'blackware' and producing a small range of terracotta country pottery wares. It is a pity they didn't expand on this range.

The Decline of Waterside Pottery

Harry tragically died in 1922, at the age of 64. This was a big blow to the pottery, because Harry was the very heart and soul of Waterside Pottery. He was the centre of the machine, sitting on his pottery wheel throne creating the very rhythm of the work amongst all the filth clay and dust. He was sorely missed. The workers must have thought a lot of him, because if you visit his grave in Burton church yard there is a plaque there dedicated to him from the workers of Waterside Pottery, which is an unusual but touching tribute to the man.

After Harry's death, Kenyon Bateson (Richard's brother and fellow soldier) was made an executive with Uncle Frank and, together, Kenyon and Frank organised and ran the business. Richard was upset about Kenyon being promoted to this role, but good throwers were in short supply and Richard had possibly filled Frank's pipe with clay one too many times in his youth! Business slowly began to decline throughout the 1920s. The once thriving jam jar trade slowly came to an end as jam jar companies started favouring glass jars in preference to clay. Hunts, the company that supplied them with a lot of work, went bankrupt. United Alkali were taken over by ICI, who used glass carboys for all their chemicals. Frank had to go back on the road to find more work.

By the 1930s business was really slow. This would not have been helped by the economic downturn caused by the worldwide Great Depression. The pottery went to a three day week for a long period during the early 1930s. Men began to be laid off, or just left for other jobs. Orders continued to decrease. Sadly the glass bottle was usurping the stoneware bottle. Glass was becoming cheaper to manufacture and it had the advantage of the fact you could see the contents. The pottery finally closed its doors in 1933. Frank and his daughter Gladys Steele continued the basket making and re-casing of old bottles until sometime during the Second World War, when their by-then only employee, Squire Taylor, the last 'wand weaver' of Black Burton, retired.

CHAPTER SIX

Bridge End Pottery and Stockbridge Pottery

Richard Bateson in the 1930s (Lancaster Guardian)

Richard had reached a crossroads. All the other potteries in Burton had closed down by this point, so if he was to remain in Burton, he was either going to have to find other work, or attempt to set up a pottery on his own. Thankfully for us, he chose the latter, which is what enables this tale to continue.

Richard bought Bridge End Pottery in Burton from former potter (but by then council road worker) Jack Coates for the tidy sum of £100 in 1933. The Coates family had run Bridge End Pottery since the 1870s until it was forced to close in 1922. The building had suffered neglect during the 10 years it had been out of use. The kiln was in such a bad state that it was deemed unusable, so Richard took it upon himself to build a new one. This was no mean feat. The kiln he built had an internal capacity of about 10ft square and had four fire mouths.

Richard had no access to any stoneware clay at Bridge End Pottery, so he had to use the Burton 'blackware', which meant terracotta pots. This would have made firing the kiln easier as terracotta is not fired as high as the stoneware. It also meant a departure from bottles, as bottles were only demanded in the more durable and non-porous stoneware clay. From a thrower's point of view, this must have been an absolute joy to him because bottles are notoriously hard to make on a wheel, due to the fact you have to open up the shape and then close it right down, so you are continually fighting the centrifugal force. Open form pots such as bowls and jugs are so much easier and more fun to make.

Richard produced a full range of terracotta pots at Bridge End Pottery, these included various sized plant pots (2.5 inch to 15 inch), jugs (1, 2 and 5 pints), large 24 inch mixing bowls, posy rings of various sizes, mugs, teapots and vases. Some of these pots were decorated with slips and they all had a transparent lead glaze applied to them. Sprig wares were also made. A sprig is a plaster casting of a decoration. Clay can be pressed into the sprig to produce repeat copies of the decoration that then would be applied to the pot. A sprigged blue & white mug and jug set made at Bridge End commemorating the 1935 silver jubilee is on display at Lancaster Museum.

During this period Richard only employed a boy to help; initially Gordon Booth and later Albert Oversby did this job. On days when it was considered not worth powering up the steam engine, one of the jobs required of these boys was to manually power a throwing wheel via a small crank situated low down at the front of the wheel. This was not one of the favourite jobs. When John Bateson (Richard's son) was a child he avoided playing anywhere near the pottery when he couldn't hear the steam engine in case his dad pulled him into the pottery to crank the wheel!

Richard Bateson throwing in the 1930s at Bridge End pottery. Gordon Booth is turning the wheel.

Richard marketed and sold his wares himself. He travelled about to the larger towns and cities such as Manchester, Liverpool, Lancaster, Preston and Leeds looking for possible outlets for his work. Customers would also turn up at Bridge End and do business with him direct.

Despite this modest existence, in 1934 Richard exhibited his work at the Royal Show in Ipswich, where he received a certificate of outstanding merit. In 1937, Richard was invited by the Council of Art and Industry to display his work and represent Britain in the *International Exposition of Art and Technology in Modern Life* exhibition in Paris. I have no idea how this came about. This was a prestigious event, attended by all major European countries. Each country had a pavilion and wanted to outshine the other countries, so a large amount of money was spent in designing the pavilions. Albert Speer designed Nazi Germany's pavilion, which was opposite the

Russian pavilion. He designed it with a strong anti-communist theme. It was quite an achievement for Richard to be invited to attend this event and I'm sure it generated interest and orders for his work, as well as giving him a certain kudos.

Richard Bateson with wares produced at Bridge End Pottery in the 1930s.
(Lancaster Guardian)

Stockbridge Pottery 1939-1944

Running Bridge End Pottery must have been hard work for Richard, as he could only afford to employ a lad to help him. Between the two of them, they were digging and processing all the clay, making the pots, shovelling the coal into the kiln to fire it, marketing the wares and distributing the goods. Despite the recognition and prestige of the 1937 Paris exhibition, the truth was Richard was struggling to make a living through this period. The continuing effects of the Great Depression cannot have helped.

In 1939 Harold Parkinson of Hornby Castle, a regular customer of the pottery, approached Richard about an idea for making plant pots for Woolworth's and other similar outlets. Harold was a rich man with successful businesses to his name and

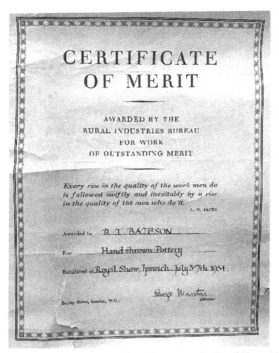

Certificate of Merit awarded to Richard Bateson at the Royal Show, 1934.

Commemorative Diploma presented to Richard Bateson at the International Exhibition of Art and Technology in Modern Life, Paris, 1937.

he was willing to invest his own money into making this venture work. Richard must have seen this as a golden opportunity to give the pottery a much needed boost. On the cusp of the Second World War, he agreed to Harold's proposals. The scheme required a larger pottery, so Waterside was leased (from William Bateson and Sons) and renamed Stockbridge Pottery (Stockbridge was the name of a mill Harold already owned) with Richard as its manager. Bridge End Pottery was given to Harold Parkinson as part of this agreement. Stockbridge Pottery then employed some of the former Waterside Pottery workers; Robert Standing (thrower), Jack Coates (formally of Bridge End – part time thrower), Charles Brayshaw (main 'taker off' for Richard), John Bateson (main 'taker off' for Robert Standing), James Singleton (clay miner), Bill Harrison (general worker and miner), Jack Telford (worker), Charlie Armer (kiln loader/unloader), Harry Capstick (worker) and Tommy Chapels ('taker off').

Robert Standing throwing at Stockbridge Pottery (the former Waterside) around 1940.

Moving back to the former Waterside Pottery meant going back to stoneware clay. The original clay mine at Waterside had become very unstable, so a new drift mine was opened. The law now required that a qualified miner had to be employed to do this, and James Singleton took the job. James had worked at

Ingleton Colliery and had also spent time in the Klondike mining for gold. I'm guessing he can't have made his fortune in the Klondike, otherwise he might have found more amenable work! After mining into the hill for 50 yards the mine collapsed. Fortunately, nobody was down at the time. The collapse was turned into an air vent, which was just as well as, when James was working down there at a later date, the mine collapsed badly near the entrance and James was able to escape through the air vent. The railway line from the old mine was dismantled and installed in the new mine, which meant James could transport the clay from the mine face to the blunger with relative ease.

One of the first major stumbling blocks encountered was that the stoneware glaze recipe used at Waterside for the last 100 years had been lost. The last man that had mixed the glaze had died and had taken the recipe to the grave with him and nobody had thought to write it down. The materials to formulate the glaze were known - but the proportions were not! In the end, Johnny Bamford, a glaze expert from Podmore's in Stoke on Trent, had to be brought in to sort out the problem. It took Johnny a few weeks to do this after firing multiple test pieces. During this time he stayed at the Joiners Arms Inn in Burton. Johnny was remembered by villagers not for solving the glaze problem, but for the fact that he was unbeatable at the billiards table!

John Bateson, Richard's son, began work in the pottery in 1941 at the age of 14. Tommy Chapels had left the pottery and Richard needed a replacement quickly, so John was pulled out of Bentham Grammar School just like Richard had been by his father many years before. John's main job was as a 'taker off' for Bob Standing. He also pugged clay and helped with the loading and unloading of the kiln.

Stockbridge Pottery, as it was now called, initially made pots similar to those Richard had been making at Bridge End Pottery, the only difference being they were now in stoneware clay. I have a very large stoneware jug that Richard made at this time and sold to the then doctor in Clapham. (I bought it when it came up for auction.) Richard would also produce one-off pots such as puzzle jugs, log-like vases (made by pressing tree bark into a wet clay cylinder), and he experimented combining the Mill Hill earthenware with the Waterside stoneware to produce agate pots (these pots were fired at the bottom of the kiln where it was cooler so that the earthenware wouldn't bloat). John Bateson could still make the cuckoo whistles (decades later, he made me one at Bentham Pottery) from 2 pinch pots that he used to make at Stockbridge Pottery. He remembers selling these to a shop in Morecambe along with posy pots and other 'fancy wares'. Surprisingly, there was still a demand for stoneware bottles, Stevens' Ink being their biggest customer. Basket casing of any large bottles was contracted out to William Bateson and Sons, now run by Gladys Steele, Frank's daughter. The pottery also picked up some large orders for 'Dig for Victory' plant pots.

Waterside/Stockbridge Pottery around 1940. Note the high crown on the third kiln, built to form a blackout during the war.

The Royal College of Art

Hitler invaded Poland on 1st September 1939. Two days later France and Britain declared war on Germany, beginning World War 2. Thankfully Richard was too old to go and fight this time. The advent of war was probably not the best time for a new business wanting to establish itself. One of the consequences of the war was the kiln chimneys had to be built up and covered, to black out the building during night firings.

In the late summer of 1940, something was about to happen that would eventually have major consequences for Richard's future career and life. The Royal College of Art (RCA) in South Kensington had been disrupted due to bombing raids. On numerous occasions the college windows had been blown out with blasts from bombs. The powers-that-be therefore decided to evacuate the whole college to somewhere safer than London. Ambleside was eventually chosen as the location and so 150 students as well as lecturers upped sticks and moved to the Lake District, where they remained for the rest of the war. The students were housed in two large hotels: the Salutation and the Queens. Spare hotel rooms and function rooms were used as classrooms.

A lot of equipment was brought up from London, but they couldn't bring heavy items such as pottery kilns. The acting head of the RCA ceramic department, Helen Pincombe, started enquiring about potteries and kilns in the area that she could possibly use to make and fire students' work. Helen heard about Stockbridge Pottery in Burton, so she visited and met up with Richard Bateson. I can only imagine she must have been blown away by Richard's throwing prowess. Richard was happy to fire RCA students' work and he was also happy to have them come over to the pottery for some work experience and teaching. I suspect the RCA were more than willing to pay something for this service. RCA students thus became regular visitors to the pottery during the war. Helen Pincombe also did some of her own work at the pottery. Richard's son John can remember Helen making two-piece moulds for the production of salt and pepper pots (in the shape of owls and cockerels) and also for cuckoo whistles. These moulds were for slip casting and this was probably the first slip casting to be done in Burton. Helen also worked on sprig moulds, carving the blanks from plaster of Paris. Richard spent some time teaching Helen and the students how to throw on the wheel. Helen must have seen the potential of Richard as a throwing teacher during these visits and stored this knowledge for future use.

Helen was the acting head of ceramics at the RCA; the actual head of ceramics, William Staite Murray, had gone on a three month trip to Rhodesia in 1940 and decided not to come back. I'm sure the war heavily influenced his decision. In the 1958 edition of Pottery Quarterly, there is a profile of Helen Pincombe in which she says:

> "College career hindered by war but acquired silver medal and was asked to stay on at Ambleside until Staite Murray returned, which he never did. Ambleside – ghastly from pottery point of view, except for brief visits to Burton-in-Lonsdale, where Mr Bateson taught me some things about throwing while he made traditional kitchen crocks."

The end of Stockbridge Pottery

Business at Stockbridge Pottery unfortunately wasn't going very well. The war probably didn't help. The Woolworths orders that Harold Parkinson had originally hoped to procure never materialised. To top it all Richard came down with pneumonia which, at the time, was a life-threatening illness, and meant he could not work for several months. Harold Parkinson, in a last-ditch attempt, put plant in for the manufacture of sewage pipes. These machines consumed the clay quicker than the men could dig and process it. Even worse, after the first firing of the pipes, it was very apparent that the Waterside clay was the wrong mixture for pipe manufacture as the pipes buckled and warped in the kilns. This could have been rectified by additions such as 'grog' (fired clay ground to a powder). This would have required time and experiment. Richard would surely have sorted it out, but unfortunately he was off work ill. Specialists from Stoke could have been brought in. John Bateson (Richard's son) thinks that by then Harold Parkinson felt he'd thrown away enough of his money into the pottery and so declared the venture bankrupt. Stockbridge Pottery ceased trading in 1944 and was the last of the Burton potteries.

CHAPTER SEVEN

A Change of Career

Carder Bros Pottery 1944–1946

Richard thankfully recovered from pneumonia and with the help of the government-run direction of labour scheme was sent to Carder Bros pottery in Brockmoor in the Midlands. Richard was employed as a thrower and Richard's son John also went as his 'taker off'. It was here that Richard proved his skill by being able to throw one-gallon bottles faster than a worker (Bill Potts) could make them using a jigger jolly machine. He was, however, beginning to find the work harder.

Teaching at the Royal College of Art, Central College of Arts and Crafts and Wimbledon School of Art 1946-1964

Around 1946 Helen Pincombe needed a throwing tutor at the RCA, now back up and running in South Kensington. She must have been reflecting on her time visiting Burton-in-Lonsdale with her students during the war and decided Richard was the ideal man for the task. She contacted Richard and offered him the job. Richard decided to accept the position.

Richard and family moved to Wimbledon and lived in Raynes Park. He began teaching at the RCA on a part-time basis. Helen Pincombe was friendly with Dora Billington, who ran the Central School of Art and Craft. Helen recommended Richard to Dora, who then invited Richard to teach part time at Central, which he accepted. Richard also took on a teaching position at Wimbledon School of Art. He ended up running the pottery course at Wimbledon.

By all accounts Richard took well to teaching. He ended up

teaching a lot of the rising stars of the studio pottery movement which was slowly emerging in the wake of the publication of *A Potter's Book* by Bernard Leach.

The students and lecturers that Richard would have encountered whilst teaching (at the Royal College of Art, Central School of Arts and Crafts; and Wimbledon School of Art) reads like a "Who's Who" of contemporary 20th century British ceramicists. This list includes: Dora Billington, Helen Pincombe, Allan Caiger-Smith, David Frith, Dan Arbeid, Ian Auld, Gordon Baldwin, George Frederick Cook, Derek Davis, Ruth Duckworth, Siddig El Nigoumi, Trefor Owen, Margaret Hine, Gillian Lowndes, Eric James Mellon, Donald Mills, William Newland, Eileen Nisbet, Peter O'Mally, Robin Welch, Rosemary Wren, Maggie Berkowitz and Ann Wyne Reeves. This list is by no way complete; these are

Contemporary studio pottery bottle shape, thrown by Richard Bateson in the 1950s or 1960s. He kept this piece close by him until the end of his life, so must have appreciated it.

just some of the people I have researched. I have tried contacting the people on this list, but sadly most searches seem to end in a *Guardian* Obituary as, at their youngest, they are going to be in their 80s. Thankfully though I have managed to contact and interview a few of Richard's former students.

Art historian Marshal Colman has done extensive research on the Central School of Art and Crafts under Dora Billington at this time. He interviewed Alan Caiger-Smith and Valentinos Charalambous (both prominent studio potters), who were taught by Richard at Central and both described him as a "lovely man". Here are some quotes referring to Richard from Marshal's blog:

"The Central in around 1950 was an old building filled with ex-servicemen and young girls, known by the students as "The Central School of Tarts and Drafts". Billington had taken on an old Yorkshire country thrower, Richard Bateson, whom Caiger-Smith found to be endlessly patient and helpful, though preferring to give advice outside the classroom where he could have a sly smoke at the same time."

"Everyone who knew him (Richard Bateson) at the Central agrees he was by far the best thrower there and Billington obviously respected and valued his skill."

"Billington had put together the team that would define the New Look in ceramics at the Central: Harding Green as her loyal lieutenant, Richard Bateson, a country potter with an extraordinary command of throwing, and two young potters, William Newland and Kenneth Clark, who were outside the Leach orbit."

Kenneth Clark (a former student and teacher from Central, who went on to design pots at Denby) recalls *"a quietly sympathetic and patient teacher".*

The Welsh potter Trefor Owen was taught by Richard at Wimbledon. Aberystwyth University Art Gallery have a biography of Owen where they mention this:

"He attended Wimbledon School of Art (1960-1963) where he was taught by Richard Bateson, one of the last surviving country potters."

I managed to contact Trefor Owen in 2020. Trefor said that Richard was a brilliant, inspirational thrower who had made a big impression on him. He can remember Richard throwing very big cider jars with ease. Trefor can also recall Richard and his students building a small scale coal-fired bottle kiln on the art school grounds.

Trefor mentioned to me that Richard taught David Frith at Wimbledon School of Art in 1962. David and Margaret Frith are very successful studio potters; they run Brookhouse Pottery in North Wales where they sell their pottery and also teach pottery classes. I was able to interview him about his experiences of being taught by Richard. David said that the reason he went to Wimbledon School of Art in the first place was because a friend of his already at the college had told him about this wonderful elderly man called "Dickie Bateson" who used to come in and teach throwing, and David was very keen to learn how to throw pots.

"Dickie was the reason I went to Wimbledon School of Art. He taught one day a week when I was there ... He was a very friendly guy. He didn't teach how I would perhaps teach people now. He would just do a demonstration. You just had to watch him and try and copy what he did ... He had a very nice personality. He used to wear a long white coat and he'd roll his sleeves up and throw a pot and he wouldn't have a spot of clay on him ... He (Richard) didn't like Bernard Leach's pots, because all Leach's pots had a wobble and Richard's never did."

Richard demonstrating the neck stage of throwing at Central School of Arts and Crafts, wearing his long white coat (complete with clay spots on this occasion)

David told me that Richard's techniques had a big influence on him. One technique that Richard taught David was how to get an initial large lift to the clay wall using his left hand. David referred to this as 'the Bateson lift', a phrase that he still uses today when he teaches his students how to do it.

A few years after David and Margaret set up their first pottery, David met Richard again. Richard was at the time working for the Rural Industries Bureau and visited Llangollen Pottery, where he was giving advice. David found out Richard was in the area and so arranged to meet him in a pub in Ruithin. David introduced his wife Margaret to Richard and explained what an amazing thrower Richard was, to which Richard replied "Well you should have seen my Dad - he could throw a hundred gallon bottles before his breakfast!"

David mentioned that, whilst working in London, Richard had damaged his wrist whilst loading a kiln. This meant that when he was throwing a bottle shape, he would get to a certain point on the collar where his wrist would suddenly click and cause a little indentation in the pot. Richard decided that, rather than remove this indentation, he would leave it in, as his trade mark. In the early 1970s, a couple of guys came into David's workshop. They were potters from "somewhere down south". They started to show David some photographs of their work which included cider bottles of various sizes amongst other pots. David looked at some of the photos of the larger cider bottles and instantly recognised them as Richard's work, indentation and all. He asked them who made these. To which they replied "Well, we've got this old guy that retired to the village and he comes in and throws these bottles for us. We don't ask him, he just comes and does it, you know". I don't think Richard could really help himself. If there was a pottery in the vicinity of his house he would be in there and at it on the wheel. Exactly the same as what happened with my mum at Bentham Pottery in 1977. We still have a few large bottle shapes that Richard threw at Bentham Pottery. I now notice the slight indentation on the collar, which I hadn't until David mentioned it.

The author with a large jug thrown by Richard Bateson at Stockbridge/Waterside Pottery in the 1940s.

Gordon Baldwin is one of the world's most distinguished sculptural potters. I managed to contact Gordon by phone at his home in Shropshire and he clearly remembers being taught by Richard in his first year at Central School of Art in 1950, when Richard was coming in one day a week to teach throwing. Gordon spoke very highly of Richard's skills on the wheel. He said that the students at Central picked up on the fact that Richard's background as a teacher at an art college hadn't followed the traditional route:

"He certainly knew how to throw! ... he was thought of as being slightly alien, because he came from a different world."

Maggie Berkowitz wrote an obituary for Richard in Ceramic Review 132 in 1991. In it she writes:

"I had always known of Burton Potteries but met Mr Bateson in 1951 when he was running the pottery department at the

Wimbledon School of Art and teaching throwing a day a week at Central School. Two northern exiles, we talked nostalgically, crouched over a wheel. He told me he'd liked throwing little things, even the 4" plant pots thrown 'off the lump' at a rate to challenge machine production … Dickie Bateson was not able to use his inherited skills to exploit the post-war market for the handmade. He was too nice to be a hard-nosed business man."

Photographs of Richard making a tall jug were included in Dora Billington's book *The Techniques of Pottery*. Also included in the book was a photo of Richard's hands entitled *The Potter's Hands*, which went on to win an international photography award and was exhibited around the world. In 1958 Richard demonstrated his method of throwing big pots to the Craftsmen Potters' Association.

Mary Wondrausch featured an interview with Richard about the Burton pottery industry in her book "On Slipware" published in 1986. Richard would have been 92 years old at the time of the interview. Mary commented that Richard still "had almost total recall of his working life". Richard went on to describe the day-to-day life of running Waterside Pottery. At the end of the article Mary goes on to say:

"Mr Bateson himself went on to teach at the Central School of Art in London, passing on his throwing skills. He worked under Dora Billington, who much admired him. Thus a whole generation of notable modern potters learnt their skills and a feel for pottery from Richard Bateson."

Richard's teaching career continued to blossom and carried him right through to the early 1960s, when education rulings from Whitehall suddenly demanded that all teachers in further education had to obtain a teaching qualification. Richard had no such qualification. The fact that he was very obviously a natural teacher with vast life experience in pottery counted for nothing.

Cover of Dora Billington's
The technique of pottery, featuring the
hands of Richard Bateson

Strangely enough, exactly the same happened to me when I was teaching pottery at Craven College in the early 2000s. I was given the same choice, which was either get the teaching qualification or leave. I was in my mid-thirties at the time, so I decided it was worth getting the teaching qualification. However, Richard would have been close to retirement at this point and I can't blame him for not wanting to go back to college to study. Richard was thus forced out of teaching. This didn't matter though, as Richard's reputation as a pottery teacher had spread around London. Amateur potters and former students were only too pleased to employ him for one-to-one lessons.

In the early 1960s, Richard moved to Assington near Sudbury in Suffolk and set up a small studio pottery, mainly for the purpose of teaching. Around this time Richard also began working for the Rural Industries Bureau, giving much advice and help to potters, both studio and industrial. He must have been missing Yorkshire though, because in 1965 he moved to Masongill, within a few miles of Burton-in- Lonsdale. In the early 1970s he moved back to Burton and it was around this time that he turned up at Bentham pottery with his grandchildren and began teaching another prominent studio potter, my mum.

Richard Bateson died at the age of 98 in 1991. He is buried in Burton-in-Lonsdale church yard with his wife Annie and their two sons, John and Henry.

Richard and Annie Bateson celebrate their platinum wedding (70 years) with their children on 10 November 1989. {Left to right) Back row: Henry Bateson, John Bateson. Front row: Margaret McKergow (nee Bateson), Richard Bateson, Annie Bateson, Peter McKergow (Margaret's husband)

Epilogue

It saddens me to think that of the five working potteries in Burton-in-Lonsdale in 1900, employing 80 or so men, none exists today. Where did the Burton potters go wrong and what could they have done to ensure a continuity of business and long-term job security?

In fairness, industrialisation of the pottery industry from the early 20th century forced the majority of traditional potteries out of business. The closest rival potteries to Burton, producing similar products in similar situations, were Chesterfield and Castleford. Both towns had several potteries, most of which closed down in the years just after the First World War.

Four of the five Burton potteries specialised in the production of stoneware bottles, when this was a product in slow decline. The Burton potteries desperately needed to find other products to sell. I feel that they had two choices - they could scale things down and produce traditional hand thrown country pottery, or they could scale things up, introduce up-to-date equipment and techniques and produce more modern industrial pottery.

Town End Pottery never actually made stoneware bottles; rather they produced traditional terracotta country pottery mainly selling to local markets. The stoneware potteries occasionally made wares in the country pottery tradition albeit usually in stoneware clay rather than terracotta. Richard proved that it was possible to make the transition from making stoneware bottles to producing a range of country pottery when he first set up on his own at Bridge End Pottery. It is possible, with the right person in charge, that any of the Burton Potteries could have gone down the country pottery route. Unfortunately, the pottery owners seemed to be stuck in their ways, reluctant to move away from making bottles and a lot of the time the children of the owners were not interested in taking over. I guess you can't blame them, as they would have seen first-hand the working conditions, hard graft and long hours required to run a pottery for often little financial reward which may understandably have been off-putting. My 16-year-old son currently feels the same way, which doesn't bode well for the longer-term continuation of Bentham Pottery. You really must have a passion for the job to make it work.

Two former Town End Pottery employees, Freddie Slater and George Kilshaw, tried to set up on their own when Jacky Parker, the owner of Town End Pottery, died in 1908. These two men both had a solid in-depth knowledge of producing country pottery and domestic wares. Sadly, neither was successful. Freddie Slater borrowed money and bought Town End Pottery. Freddie was one of the best throwers to emerge from Burton. Unfortunately, this didn't translate into him being brilliant at business and he went bankrupt within a few years, just before the First World War. George Kilshaw bought or rented Greta Bank Pottery in 1907. However, he only lasted until 1910 before going bankrupt.

Wetherigg's Pottery (Penrith) and Soil Hill Pottery (Halifax) are two examples of historic country-ware potteries that kept going long after the First World War, with Soil Hill closing in 1980 and Wetherigg's lasting until 2008.

Richard ran Bridge End Pottery as a country pottery from 1933 until 1939. Had he stayed at Bridge End and got through the war years, the pottery would surely have started to take off. After the war, there was a boom in demand for hand thrown pottery. This demand was due to two reasons:

- The large pottery manufacturers had been forced into making plain glazed utility wares during the war. This was because decorated pots required a lot of man hours and additional fuel costs, which was seen as an unnecessary luxury when men were required to fight and resources were scarce. These utility restrictions continued after the war until 1952. Hand thrown pottery with any colour or decoration became a welcome alternative to this plain industrial pottery.

- The studio pottery movement perhaps best encapsulated by Bernard Leach and The Leach Pottery at St Ives came of age after the war. The public developed an increasing interest in buying handmade pottery and also a desire to attend classes to learn how to make pots. Studio pottery was showcased in the 1951 Festival of Britain, which had a huge impact on public tastes. Interestingly, the Leach Pottery had struggled through the 1930s (just like Richard) and had come very close to bankruptcy; it was only after the war that they started to do well.

If Richard had remained at Bridge End it is possible that he could have ridden the crest of the studio pottery wave and firmly established both Bridge End Pottery and his reputation as an outstanding thrower. I feel sure that prospective studio potters would have been queuing up to visit Bridge End Pottery to try to get an apprenticeship with him, in the same way that students sought apprenticeships at the Leach Pottery. Bernard Leach may well have had the art school background and the writing skill, but there can be no dispute that Richard was by far the better thrower. Richard's children Margaret, John or Henry could then possibly have taken over the pottery? However, this is all hypothetical and the Royal College students would still have descended on Richard during the war and later attempted to whisk him away to London.

To go down the modern industrial pottery route, the potteries needed to invest money in new skills and equipment. Robert Bateson was Harry and Frank's brother. Remember Robert? He split from William Bateson and Sons in 1902, because he felt the business wasn't going in the right direction and needed to modernise. Robert was paid out and he bought another pottery, Greta Pottery in Burton and set up on his own. Could Robert be the man to make these changes? He did purchase a large dish making jigger and jolly and also a large filter press for drying out the clay. The filter press would have been a new concept in 1902 and it effectively did away with the need for the clay settling pans.

So, it looked like Robert was doing the right things and heading in the right direction. However tragically he died six years later and his dreams were unfortunately unrealised.

In my opinion, in order to become a modern industrial pottery the following needed to happen:

- Move away from bottles and concentrate instead on kitchenware/household pots
- Move away from throwing. Harry and Richard wouldn't have liked that
- Invest in jiggers and jollys for producing plates, mugs, bowls and simple shapes
- Invest in a plaster workshop so they could make their own moulds for the jigger and jolly wheels, but also so they could make moulds for slip casting things like teapots
- Invest in slip casting equipment
- Employ a ceramic designer
- Employ people to decorate pots
- Introduce a range of glazes
- Move away from single firing and introduce bisque firing.

I guess that's quite a lot of things that needed to be done and they would have had to import people with some of these skills, probably from Stoke. However, it needn't have happened all at once. Ideally, they needed to be slowly investing in all this in the boom years before the First World War.

Neither Richard nor Harry was, realistically, ever going to make these changes. Throwing pots was in their blood and there was no way that they were going to give up on using the pottery wheel. In my opinion the men that could have made these changes were Frank or Robert (or possibly Kenyon). It really is a great shame that Frank and Harry couldn't have taken on some of Roberts's ideas and worked in partnership with him, instead of having to pay him out.

I feel Richard failed at Stockbridge Pottery because he was trying to run a modern industrial pottery with techniques from the previous century. Harold Parkinson had the money, but not the right team or knowledge to make a success of it. Richard would have done far better to have remained at Bridge End employing a few workers producing country pottery wares. I keep coming back to this point! However, that is easy for me to say in retrospect.

There are examples of potteries that produced stoneware bottles and successfully managed to transform into a modern industrial pottery. Denby Pottery was exclusively making bottles in 1900. Today it is a very successful industrial pottery producing tableware and distributing it all over the world. In 2015 Denby employed 707 people and had a turnover of £46.5 million. When I visited Denby in 2018, they had just taken on 50 young apprentices to help cope with the demand for pots, particularly from abroad. Imagine what the impact of a similar successful pottery could have had on Burton-in-Lonsdale and the surrounding area?

Pearson's and Co of Chesterfield was one of the biggest manufacturers of stoneware bottles in the country. They managed to make the transition from bottles to producing a range of tableware. Interestingly their tableware designs were really based on the stoneware bottles. The pots they produced used the same glazes and same 'copper' tops as on the bottles and they also used the same lettering technique that they had used for branding the bottles to make a range of named pots. Waterside Pottery would have done well to have learned from Pearson's, as this would have been easier to implement, as they already knew these techniques. Pearson's and Co kept going until 1994, when they went bankrupt. I think the reason they went out of business was they didn't introduce new products but stayed with the same ones. The lesson being that any pottery really has to adapt to the fashions and tastes of the time. If Bentham Pottery had just continued producing the wares we were making in the 1970s we would no longer be in business today.

I also feel that the Burton potteries were a bit remote from the ceramic heartland of Stoke-on-Trent. This meant that it was harder to keep abreast of any changes in techniques and skills that were vital to their continuity. It also meant that new skills really had to be imported from Stoke, which would have been hard to implement, not least because of the upheaval required to move up to Burton.

Finally I feel strongly that Burton didn't make use of their women folk. Pottery in Burton was an exclusive male occupation, with the exception of Mable and Millie working as jam jar makers in the First World War. In contrast Stoke employed thousands of women in their potteries, mainly as designers and decorators. In my experience of selling pots, it is mainly women that choose them. Surely it makes sense then to involve them in the design, making and decorating process?

Today sadly no potteries remain in Burton. Bentham Pottery and Ingleton Pottery are nearby, both of which have run successfully over the last 40 years or so, based upon a scaled down studio pottery model, not dissimilar from what Richard was doing at Bridge End (although we aren't digging our own clay and shovelling the 12 tons of coal into the kiln to fire it!).

Was Richard upset about the fact he couldn't retain the Burton pottery industry? My feelings are that he was heartbroken at the time Stockbridge Pottery closed in 1944. However, I really feel he found his true vocation in life teaching throwing, where he could demonstrate his unquestionable throwing skills to appreciative audiences at the same time as talking – both of which are things he loved to do.

Appendices

Origin of the name Black Burton

Burton-in-Lonsdale used to be known as Black Burton. Most people think this was due to the amount of smoke arising from the coal-fired kilns of the local pottery industry. However, Stoke had far more potteries than Burton and it was never referred to as Black Stoke.

A far more likely, though understandably less popular, reason for the 'black' prefix was due to the morals of the people living there. The potteries would have employed a lot of men and it would have brought a concentration of young men into the area working in what were essentially small scale pottery factories. The potters were fiercely competitive with each other and with the other potteries. Added to this was the fact that miners from the collieries around Ingleton would have lived in Burton as well as cotton/silk mill workers and farmers. Is it possible that these men perhaps could have introduced 'black' habits such as an over-indulgence in alcohol, non-attendance at church, blasphemous language and cock fighting? There were certainly as many pubs as potteries in the village. Here are some extracts from the Lancaster Guardian of 21st August 1875 perhaps confirming this view, though diplomatically defending the morals of the then 'present' potters.

> *"Without any intention to make the Burtonians of a past generation more vile than their neighbours, it may be said that rudeness and cruelty were mixed up with many of their amusements."*

The article goes on:

"Cock fighting was the crowning sin and the most brutalising practice of the past generation . . . This love of cock fighting led to much drinking, quarrelling and dishonesty. There was such a demand for fighting cocks that the immediate neighbourhood could not meet it and consequently it was a risk for anybody to keep a game cock within a dozen miles of Burton. Some of the lovers of this inhuman diversion, when a 'gam cock', as it was called, had been sighted set at defiance locks and bars, law and parish constables. Some of these game cock stealers were known to travel as far away as Kellet, Sedbergh and Nook near Kendal, and as many as 17 cocks have been the fruits of one night's plunder. The stolen cocks used to be kept in the potteries, and, for a time, covered under large pots."

"Rudeness of speech and unmannerly conduct at Burton-in-Lonsdale are now, comparatively speaking, a thing of the past. There was a time when few persons, especially on a Sunday, could enter the village without being called some offensive name."

"The potter's song of the past would not apply to the present class of potter:

   The Bull (inn) will break all the Burton pots
   and drink the Fountain (inn) dry.
   It will turn the Punch Bowl (inn) wrong side up
   and make the Hen and Chicken (inn) fly."

A third possible reason for the name Black Burton, and I have to admit that this is my own theory, is that the local terracotta clay, dug up at Mill Hill near Greeta House and used by all the Burton potteries, is in its raw processed state black in colour. The Burton potters used to refer to it as 'blackware'. When you dig it from Mill

Hill (and I have done this numerous times) it is a grey colour. It only turns black when you process it by grinding it down, turning it into a thin liquid, passing it through a sieve and then drying it out again. The photo below is of freshly-thrown Burton 'blackware'. I am told that the reason the clay is black is because it has oil in it, which I'm guessing would contribute to fuel in the firing process. The clay throws really well and fires to a light red colour.

Could the unusual colour of the clay contribute to the 'black' of Black Burton. I will let you decide that one. Let's face it, it's better than the 'morals of the people' option! Mind you, Burton upon Trent is famous for producing Marmite and they don't call it Black Burton because of that.

Freshly thrown Burton 'blackware'

Town End Pottery

Burton sometime after 1837 (as Stone Bower house is built/visible). Greta Pottery, Bridge End Pottery and the Bradshaw Pottery are visible in the foreground. The bottle kiln of Town End Pottery is just visible at the top right hand side.

The bottle kiln of Town End Pottery can be seen on the top right-hand side of this drawing of Burton-in-Lonsdale (on the way out towards Ingleton). It is the only image of Town End Pottery I have ever seen, which is surprising, considering the pottery was still in business up to the First World War. Somebody out there must have some photos?

Town End Pottery was an old established pottery that can be traced back to the 1700s. At the dawn of the 20th century, it was run by John "Jacky" Parker. Jacky had inherited the business from his father William Parker who had bought the pottery in 1863. Jacky was a hardworking man and a good thrower. He produced traditional country wares all in terracotta (or 'blackware' as the Burton potters called it) and sold his pots locally. He would have made such things as jugs, jars, bowls, butter pots, plant pots and basically any pot that was demanded by households or farms. The pots probably had a simple slip decoration. The clay would have all been taken from Mill Hill, close to Greeta House.

The main throwers were Jacky Parker and Freddie Slater. Freddie learnt how to throw at Town End Pottery and became one of the best throwers to emerge from Burton. Tom Park, a blind man, was employed as a wheel turner, which would basically involve sitting on a seat and turning a hand crank to power a pottery wheel. George Kilshaw, Tom Skeates and Bill or John Saul were employed as general workers. Jacky's son Jim Parker also worked at the pottery as a youngster, but to the disappointment of Jacky showed no interest in being a potter and got out of the business as soon as he could.

Jacky used a red lead glaze on his pots. He was very fond of chewing tobacco and is remembered glazing his pots with red lead covering his hands and waistcoat then dipping his red hands into his waistcoat to grab some tobacco to chew. Nobody knew the dangers of eating raw lead at this time!

Town End Pottery had a shop where wares were on sale, so people could call in to buy and order pots. However, Jacky's main business was selling pots in Kendal, which was a regular trip. I'm guessing that he probably had a market stall in Kendal and possibly supplied some shops? He kept two horses both called Bob and a large cart for taking the pots to Kendal. Jim Brennand was one of a few people that would take the horse and cart up to Kendal. The fully laden cart would set off the night before and stay overnight at Aynams, which allowed the horses some rest before making the return journey the next day.

Sadly, Jacky died at the age of 64 and on his 64th birthday in 1908. It is thought that he died of lead poisoning.

Freddie Slater borrowed money and bought the business. However, despite Freddie being a brilliant thrower, he wasn't great at business. According to Richard Bateson, he was "too busy advising other people how to run their businesses, instead of running his own". Freddie only lasted three or four years before going bankrupt just before the First World War. Freddie then moved out of Burton and got a job at Portobello Pottery in Edinburgh, where he discovered lots of new pottery techniques, trade unions and health & safety regulations all of which he brought back to Burton-in-Lonsdale when he eventually returned, causing all sorts of disruption within the Burton potteries; that story is covered in the main text.

Unlike the other potteries in Burton at this time, Town End Pottery did not produce stoneware bottles. This could have been because they had no access to digging the stoneware clay, or it could be that they had simply found a good market for the country wares that they produced?

I've often wondered whether if Jacky's son Jim had shown more interest in the business, the pottery would have continued for longer. After all, Wetheriggs Pottery, a family-run pottery near Penrith, produced similar wares to Town End Pottery and managed to keep going until 2008. The truth is that pottery is a very fickle business and it requires at least one dedicated person willing to work long hours for sometimes little remuneration. It's often easier to find other work. Interestingly, Jim Parker's son, John Willy Parker ended up working at Waterside Pottery after the war, so it would appear that the pottery gene seems to have skipped a generation. Jacky had daughters, who I guess could have continued the business; unfortunately, pottery in Burton was seen as an exclusively male activity. I have never heard of any women potters in Burton, although Richard Bateson's sister and sister-in-law, Mable and Millie, did work briefly at Waterside Pottery during the First World War when the pottery lost a lot of its men to the war effort. Richard can remember being "rather horrified to think of women in the pottery" when he found out whilst he was in the army. Richard was concerned not just about the dirty conditions in the pottery, but also the foul language used by the potters.

Town End Pottery was sadly demolished by the council in 1923 in order to widen the road. Did I mention I have no photos of it?

The Coates Pottery, aka the Baggaley Pottery, aka Bridge End Pottery

The Coates Pottery in 1919. (Left to right) unknown, Jack Coates, Cliff Priestley, Thomas Coates, Bob Saul, Bill Saul, Jack Bradshaw.

The Coates family were the big rival pottery family to the Batesons at the turn of the 20th century.

Four generations of the Baggaley family ran the pottery prior to the Coates family buying it in 1887. The Baggaley family also owned the Punch Bowl Inn in Burton and rather craftily used to pay their workers on a Friday night over the inn bar.

Earthenware household pots were originally produced here, using the Mill Hill 'blackware'. The Coates family introduced stoneware for the manufacture of bottles, dug open cast from where the football pitch is now.

The hearsay of two potters talking in the mid-1970s would have it that the Coates family originally came from Liverpool, where they ran a public house. As a side-line they would sell liquor without tax paid on it to other pubs. It was while selling such substances that they came into contact with the Baggaley family at the Punch Bowl Inn and ended up marrying into the

Baggaley family and thus the pottery. However that is just hearsay!

The head of the Coates family was Thomas or "Old Dine" as he was called. Thomas Coates was by all accounts a good potter and a good business man, which is a rare combination. He made a lot of money from pottery and bought a lot of property in Burton. He bought the Bradshaw Pottery in 1886 and immediately closed it down and converted it into houses. This was probably a strategic step to eliminate competition. He bought Greta Pottery in 1879 and ran it in tandem with the Coates Pottery.

Richard Bateson recounts a tale involving Thomas Coates and the River Greta running dry in his memoir:

"In the late 1860s, workmen on their way to their jobs at the Waterside Pottery and the hands who worked at the Greta Cotton Mill found that there was little or no water running from above Burton Bridge. The water which drove the large mill wheel and machinery ceased to flow. Imagine the consternation of the fifty or sixty workers from Burton, Bentham and district.

"T' beck's dry!" would go round the whole district.

I think it was the Towlers, who had taken over from the Smitties, who were working the mill at that time, and of course were mainly responsible for the upkeep of the weir which used to be some fifty yards below the bridge. After investigation, it was found that a large hole had formed in the river bed, about three hundred yards upstream, into which practically all the water was disappearing.

I can remember that we used to learn to swim in this hole, which was about ten feet deep. It was always called George Hole – and still retains that name. I have often wondered why. Was a boy called George perhaps drowned there in some past forgotten time? The name was handed down to us from our parents.

Now as to the hole appearing in the river-bed – the explanation was very simple. In the early eighteenth and nineteenth centuries, the Hodgsons and Sargentsons who owned the mineral rights had decided to sink a new coal shaft at Wilson Wood (just below Ingleton), but they were afraid of water that might enter from old workings. They decided to drain these old workings. To do this, and to arrive at an adequate lead to drain the water, they had to start over a mile downstream, in the entrance to Clifford Woods. Part of the level had to be run beneath the river – and it was here, at George Hole, that the water was disappearing.

Tom Baggaley Coates, who owned the Baggaley Pottery, came to the rescue. He blocked up the level by ramming down into one of the level-shaft some bales of cotton from the mill.

At approximately every two to three hundred yards, a shaft was sunk into the level, partly for air, and also to wind out spare soil or clay. The first air hole was in the field beyond Greta Pottery. This was the one that was blocked by T.B.Coates to enable water to flow into its proper course and bank up at the weir to turn the wheel at Greta Cotton Mill."

Another tale of Thomas Coates can be found in *Pottery in Lunesdale* by Jean M. Robinson:

"Thomas Coates, who took over the Baggaley pottery from Thomas Baggaley, fought an action at Leeds Assizes which had been brought against him by the man who lived next door to the pottery, Levi Towler. The latter contended that the collecting of reddle (clay) by men who worked at the pottery was undermining his hedge, and furthermore he claimed it was malice on the part of Thomas Coates. The action cost Coates over £1000 in solicitors' (Pearson and Pearson, Kirkby Lonsdale) and witnesses' fees, but he won the case, being awarded Levi Towler's house in payment."

Thomas's son Jack Coates inherited the pottery on Thomas's death. Jack managed to keep the pottery going until 1923 when depleting orders for stoneware bottles forced him to close. Jack ended up working on the roads for Settle Rural District Council as a lines man. He did return to throwing briefly in the 1940s to work for Richard at Stockbridge Pottery.

Richard Bateson bought the pottery in 1933 for £100 and worked it until 1939.

Greta Pottery

Greta Pottery about 1905. (Left to right) Bert Williams, William Bateson (son of Robert Bateson), Bob Law, Bob Saul the boy (he is hard to see), John Atkinson, Richard Bateson (son of Robert Bateson).

Greta Pottery was founded in 1843 by William Bateson. The pottery was taken over by James Kilburn in 1860. The main product of the pottery was stoneware bottles. Kilburn was the only Burton potter to mark his wares *J Kilburn, manufacturer, Burton-in-Lonsdale*. Thomas Coates bought the pottery following Kilburn's death in 1879. Robert Bateson, formally of William

Bateson and Sons, bought the pottery from Thomas Coates in 1902. Robert Bateson introduced new jigger and jolly machines as well as a filter press. A filter press would have been a modern piece of equipment at this time and it effectively did away with the need for clay settling pans. Robert had a lot of ideas about developing the pottery into a more modern industrial pottery. Unfortunately, his ideas were never realised due to his untimely death in 1908. Robert's eldest son Ernest took on the pottery for a few years before selling it to William Bateson and Sons. The pottery was then stripped of all its machinery, which was taken to Waterside Pottery, and the building was sold to Wilfred Waggett on the condition that it would never again be used for manufacturing pottery.

William Bateson, the man that originally built Greta Pottery, had two sons called Richard (not our Richard – let's call him Cousin Richard, as he was a distant cousin) and James. I'm not sure why they didn't inherit the business from their father – maybe William had to sell it for financial reasons. Cousin Richard and James did, though, become highly skilled potters in their own right, working at both Greta Pottery and Waterside Pottery. Richard remembers them very fondly, as they used to come into Waterside Pottery on occasions, after they had retired, to throw pots. Richard can remember, with some degree of shame, dripping engine oil onto James' cap through the floorboards on the second floor whilst James was throwing downstairs. Richard always spoke with a high degree of reverence about Cousin Richard:

> *"I wish I could have carried on in the way Richard Bateson did. He was one of the cleverest potters that I think this village has ever had in terms of colours, ideas, decoration and experiments. It's a pity that he couldn't have had a free hand. He was no business man in any shape or form, but he was just an artist, a pottery artist and a country pottery artist too. A man full of inventiveness. Wonderful chap."*

The Dalesman magazine of March 1949 mentions this Cousin Richard:

> *"Richard worked mainly at Waterside. He lived to a good old age, and is remembered as a lovable man, called affectionately 'Uncle Dick'- a skilled craftsman, maker of many ornamental garden pots to be seen in local gardens."*

Greta Bank Pottery

The Greta Bank Pottery was situated on the North Bank of the River Greta one mile east of Burton at Barnoldswick, or Barnawick as it is usually pronounced (and sometimes spelt). The pottery is thought to have been built around the 1850s.

Greta Bank Pottery is first mentioned in the Lancaster Guardian on 19th February 1859:

> *"Stoneware Pottery, at Barnawick, within 2 miles of High Bentham, lately in the occupation of Mr Thomas Greenup, with five cottages on the premises, and the tolls of the bridge over the river Greta. There is an abundance of excellent clay on the land."*

And from the same paper dated 1st January 1869:

> *"Mr James Parker of Greta Bank, Barnoldswick, required the men and boys in his employ at the Stone Bottle Works with a good supper."*

James Parker, followed by his son James Parker (Junior), worked the pottery until 1887 when it was bought by William Bateson (of William Bateson & Sons, Richard's grandfather). William had been working for James Parker Junior prior to him buying the pottery.

William Bateson & Sons bought Waterside Pottery in 1888 and

worked both Greta Bank Pottery and Waterside Pottery in
tandem for a time. They then decided to rebuild and expand
Waterside Pottery (from one to three kilns) in the late 1890s.
Greta Bank Pottery enabled them to continue manufacturing
pottery whilst the builders were enlarging Waterside Pottery.
Greta Bank Pottery was worked until Waterside Pottery was
completed in 1905. It then stood idle for two years, until 1907
when it was taken over by George Kilshaw, a former Town End
Pottery employee who worked the pottery with Gamaliel Briscoe
as the main thrower. Stoneware bottles were mainly made here
with some domestic and country ware. Unfortunately, Kilshaw
went bankrupt in 1910 and with that the pottery finally closed.

I have no idea when the pottery was knocked down. However a
small section of the outer kiln wall (hovel wall) still remains. This
is the last physical remnant of the Burton potteries past (in terms
of buildings).

Greta Bank Pottery with smoking kiln, and Penny Bridge.

Teaching to throw by Richard Timperley Bateson

This passage is taken from a short autobiographical memoir left by Richard Bateson, the last potter of Black Burton. It is a fascinating glimpse into the mind of a skilled thrower of pottery and a gifted teacher, in his own words.

I did not realise how difficult it was to put over to a student, until I had to teach the actual movements. For a long time, when helping a student, it was easier to actually continue her shape, than to tell her what to do, and how to hold her fingers when shaping. My fingers, or my brain, were telling me what I was trying to do.

If you wish to be a really competent thrower, the shape (which must of course be rounded) must be seen first of all by the brain, and then transferred to the fingers. The initial cylinder, from which most pottery shapes grow, must be in the correct position to make the final shape. Clay is naturally weathered, mixed into a 'slip', and then allowed to dry naturally. The small colloidal particles of which it is formed lie in a horizontal formation. The silicon alumina, carbon, and trace elements of which it is composed, if mixed too much by being put through a pugmill more than once, are disturbed in colloidal position, so making the clay 'short' and not easy to manage.

When I first began work, we had two regular throwers, and it is difficult to believe the speed at which these two men worked. It was always fascinating to watch a five- or six-gallon bottle being made in the time of four or five minutes. One lift or course to the cylinder, and one knuckling course to the full lift and width to the gauge, leaving a sufficient roll of clay to run in the top and make the neck. The width of the corkhole was gauged by the fingers: two fingers' width for the ordinary bottle, and three fingers' width for a treacle-jar. The amount of clay required was approximately five pounds for a half-gallon, eleven pounds or a Hyndburn brick for one gallon, and an extra brick for each of the succeeding gallons up to the six-gallon bottles. I have managed to make up to ten gallons, just once for a special order.

I have known times when I have really felt I was fighting and forcing the clay to the shape required. The bench-hand often got the blame for not wedging his clay properly. Of course the reason could be explained in several ways.

Firstly, it could be accounted for partly by the clay's having been taken from the entrance of the settling-pan, where the heavier particles in the clay had settled, resulting in less plasticity.

Secondly, after it had been housed and put into store, the clay-house man might have stiffened it by adding a dry clay which had not had time to mix thoroughly together. The colloidal particles were not fitting together in unison and the thrower was in fact working two types of disunited clay, which were not in agreement – fighting one another, in fact.

This tended to make the clay crack or tear, and it would not stretch with the smoothness required.

Thirdly, often the final excuse, and generally the real reason, would be that the thrower himself was not in the humour, and had not the patience to work with the clay as it was. Or it could be that he was not using the wheel-speed required. It is not easy to find the exact fault and to apply the correct remedy. Some days, it would be a pleasure to throw. At other times, try as one could, nothing would go right or work with rhythm. The harder one tried, the more difficult it would become. Then suddenly one would find the rhythm, and work to make the article desired, with real pleasure.

In this article, I am talking about red earthenware and stoneware clays. But clays are not quite the same, and prepared white china bodies are not often suitable to throw.

I have been telling you how I learnt to throw. I must now try to tell you how I attempted to teach students how to control and make the clay 'behave itself'.

The first essential is that clay must be mixed to the consistency required. This is generally ascertained by pressing the thumb into the lump of clay which you have previously wedged, kneaded and rolled, until it is perfectly mixed.

Next, the wheel must rotate anticlockwise, and the centre of it must not be too dry, and not wet. The ball of clay must then be placed firmly into the centre of the wheel, and (in picking up the ball) it must not be wet or slippery. This enables it to stick to the wheel's iron head, which is rotating, if possible, at about 120 revolutions per minute.

Then we have to make the ball of clay which has been placed on the wheel run perfectly. To do this, the left hand is placed firmly on the clay and the right hand is then placed on the clay with the fingers overlapping and the tips of both of your thumbs touching each other. (For your first attempt, the piece of clay should not be any larger than, say, a pint pot.)

The fingers, thumbs and the ball of the hand must surround and be adding a gradual squeezing pressure to the clay. At first, the greatest pressure must be downward, by the base of the thumb. This makes the clay adhere firmly to the wheel. Then add side-pressures by tending to close the hands, letting the finger of the right hand slide further over the left hand. If this movement is done correctly, the clay will be squeezed upward into a solid but narrow shape. Do not press too much in any one place, but narrow the circumference as you follow up the solid lump, which will now form a cone.

Then place the balls of the thumbs upon the top of the cone, and press in a downward movement, thus bringing the clay to overlap, but let it sink into itself. To the beginner, this movement has to be achieved time after time, until he feels that the clay is responding to the pressures and he is able to control it and make it run perfectly true.

Several different methods can be used for the next process, which is to bore into the centre of the spinning clay. I advise the beginner to press downwards and towards the palm – thus forming a cup-shaped hollow in the clay. Now raise the right hand slowly, still keeping a light pressure upon the clay with the thumb. The clay wall will rise with the hand.

Slacken the speed of the wheel a little. Remember – the clay MUST be running perfectly true.

Insert the fingers of the left hand into the low cylinder. Bend the knuckle of the forefinger of the right hand and press it against the tips of the fingers of the inside hand. As soon as you feel that the clay is thinning with the squeezing pressure, begin an upward movement, and you will feel that the walls of the cylinder are moving upward. Do not press too hard in one place, or you will press the clay in two! Remember, in raising a cylinder, the two pressures have to be equal.

The making of a correct cylinder is the basis of all 'thrown' shapes, whether the finished product be tall or wide. This is the first knuckling course, and it has to be practised constantly, until one is able to form a perfectly true and even cylinder, positioned ready for whatever shape he is hoping to produce. He must not be satisfied with any shape that appears, but he must endeavour to transmit to the clay the shape for whatever shape that is in his mind, through his fingers. Thus, he is knuckling and lifting the wall of clay to the desired result.

To me, the correct method, as taught by past generations, is to insert the left hand or arm into the inside of the cylinder, press outward with the tips of the fingers, and resist with the knuckle of the first finger, thus starting to gather and thin the thicker clay at the base of the wall. Then, by turning the knuckle over on to the inside fingers, the tension between the fingers and knuckle lifts, and so the shape grows into the position required.

If this can be done in one single movement, one puts life and vigour into the finished pot. Very few throwers ever reach this stage – but it should be their aim. Sometimes a little touch from the inside could have been given just to have helped the rhythm and to have made a perfect shape.

To appreciate the movement of the thrower's hands when he is working is very difficult. Once can only judge really when you see the article being actually shaped. Even when one sees it on television, the inside hand cannot be seen resisting the pressure and lifting the thinning wall of clay into the position required.

Remember, in good throwing, the walls of clay, even in a large pot or bread-mug, must not be uneven – or down it will collapse. Whenever possible – and in making smaller pieces – the inside and outside hands must touch each other. This helps to provide better unison and feeling of the balance between the two.

Acknowledgements

I could not have written any of this without help from the following people:

Richard Bateson and Henry Bateson (Richard's younger son) – I conducted extensive interviews with Richard and Henry during 1987 when I was writing my thesis on the Burton potteries for my 3D design degree at Sunderland Polytechnic.

John Bateson (Richard's older son) – I met John at Henry Bateson's funeral in 2001. John became a regular annual visitor to Bentham Pottery. It was through conversations with John that I wrote the original *Last Potter of Black Burton* essay.

Margaret McKergow, nee Bateson (Richard's daughter) – Margaret had a roll of film in her Kodak brownie with some holiday snaps on. To finish the film she took some shots of Waterside/Stockbridge Pottery around 1940. She wasn't thinking of making a visual recording of pottery in Burton at the time, however unintentionally this is exactly what she did and I am very grateful to her. Many of those photographs are included in this book.

Mark McKergow (Richard's grandson) – Mark has been a huge help in the production of this book. He has shared all his treasured Burton pottery and Richard Bateson related documents and photographs. And as well as writing the foreword, he has organised the publication as well as providing lots of encouragement.

Jo Lake (John Bateson's daughter) – I am grateful to Jo for helping John with his annual pilgrimage to Ingleton, where he would visit me at Bentham Pottery and reminisce about the Burton potteries.

Marshal Colman – Marshal very generously shared all the information he had on Richard's time teaching in London, particularly at the Central College of Arts and Crafts.

Susan Gregory – Susan suggested that I should write up this in the first place after a talk I did on the Burton Potteries. Susan has proved invaluable in suggesting research and helping with the captions on some of the photos.

Jenny Cartledge – My wife has proved invaluable in helping correct some of my grammar, spelling mistakes and random capitalisations. She has also been a sounding board for ideas and she has put up with my obsession with the Potteries of Burton.

I never actually met Jimmy Skeates, but I do feel I know him. Henry taped Jimmy and Richard talking about their early years at Waterside Pottery, sometime in the late 1970s. Henry gave me copies of these tapes and they have proved invaluable when writing this book.

About the author

Lee Cartledge is a second-generation potter, working in partnership with his mother Kathy Cartledge at Bentham Pottery, North Yorkshire, a mile from Burton-in-Lonsdale. Lee learnt his craft from his mother, who had in turn been taught by Richard Bateson as well as other people. Lee has a degree in ceramics from Sunderland Polytechnic.

Bentham Pottery has supplied its wares to galleries, craft shops, businesses and events, and has exhibited at various venues around the country, including the Victoria and Albert Museum. As well as making pots, Lee and Kathy's pottery throwing courses are greatly in demand and they have been teaching for many years.

Lee lives with his wife Jenny and son Jed in the village of Ingleton nearby the pottery.

CPSIA information can be obtained
at www.ICGtesting.com
Printed in the USA
LVHW022245180121
676820LV00030B/689

9 781789 631838